Dog Tricks

Dog Tricks

Capt. Arthur J. Haggerty
and Carol Lea Benjamin

Drawings by Carol Lea Benjamin and
Photographs by Richard Cordes

HOWELL BOOK HOUSE INC.

230 Park Avenue, New York, N.Y. 10169
Seventh Printing —1989

Library of Congress Cataloging in Publication Data

Haggerty, Arthur J
    Dog tricks.

    1. Dogs—Training.   I. Benjamin, Carol Lea, joint
author.   II. Cordes, Richard.   III. Title.
SF431.H214   636.7'08'87
ISBN 0-87605-517-X (Previously published under ISBN 0-385-13493-2)
Library of Congress Catalog Card Number 77–16919

To Babette Haggerty and Victoria Halboth

Acknowledgments

These tricks have been checked from the point of view of health and safety by:
Lyle C. Goodnow, D.V.M., Gardiner Animal Hospital, Gardiner, New York
Victor J. Schwartz, D.V.M., Hudson Valley Animal Hospital, Nyack, New York
Peter A. Segall, D.V.M., Hudson Valley Animal Hospital, Nyack, New York
Harold M. Zweighaft, D.V.M., Tri-Boro Animal Hospital, Bronx, New York

The authors wish to express their appreciation to Jim Menick, Judith Nelson, Mimi Kahn, Marie Durso, David L. Geisinger, Ricki Linsky, Laurie Nelson, Jerry Brown, Susan Zaretsky, Dr. Barbara Koopman, Jean Shishito, Richard John Sydenham, Gary Pillarsdorf, Bernard Cohen, Bob Boyle, Billie McFadden, Ben J. Mullins, Roz Shulman, Helen Hein, John Rendel, Elizabeth Epstein, Michael A. Braverman, Mark Satine, Mel Chase, Robert C. Blauser, and Tom.

Contents

Report
Sneeze
"Nothing" Trick

Introduction

The reasoning behind this book is quite simple. In our view, dogs have become part of the nation's unemployed population. The functions they have been bred for remain in their genes—Sheepdogs, having a paucity of flocks to tend, nip at children's overalls and chase after cars. Many a Shepherd, Doberman, or Rottweiler will plant himself between his owner and an awaited foe, or charge furiously at the door when a stranger approaches. Retrievers become electrified at the sight of game, Terriers still tend to chase squirrels, and Pointers still point, even before they're out of diapers. But most dogs have become indulged pets, a fine beginning, but nothing more. They are bored, sometimes to the point where they get destructive or lick away endlessly at their own paws in sheer frustration. Their fine minds, still largely a mystery to us, go unused. Or they begin their education with obedience work and never go on to graduate school.

Dogs need something to do. They want to feel useful. They love to work for praise and to feel accomplished. Sitting around and decorating the hearth isn't quite enough. Tricks can be a useful and entertaining addition to your dog's education. They will satisfy his yearnings for attention and intellectual achievement. They will allow him to be of real service to you and will help him to satisfy his unspoken longing to work. If you don't have a flock of sheep or acres full of rodents, if you don't ride to the hounds or have an estate or barge to be guarded, if you love your dog and he has little or nothing to do, this book is for you. Don't take our word for it. Just ask your dog.

But you're busy, and why should you put all this work into a pet? We know that you need some gratification, too. First, you will see marvelous changes in the dog you love. He will get brighter, more interesting, he will shine with intelligence. You will learn how to communicate with him on a finer and higher level—and he will learn to listen and to communicate with you. You, not only he, will get attention and praise. Inside you, there's a ham waiting to break into show business. With your trick dog as a sidekick, you can do it. You can entertain in your living room or on the stage. How far you take it is entirely up to you. So don't let your sleeping dog lie—wake him up and teach him some tricks!

If you love the idea of higher education for your dog, he will need a grounding in obedience work—work he needs anyway to be a good member of your household. He'll need to learn the commands HEEL, SIT, DOWN, COME, STAY, and OKAY, preferably both on and off a leash. These basic commands are not included in this trick book. After basic training, you can begin trick work and make him a comedian, a helper, a playmate for your kids. He can save you time, earn you money, protect your home, and even save your life. He can learn to walk on two feet, front or back, and take breathtaking jumps and land on his feet. He can give you his paw. He can give you a good laugh. He can give you more pleasure than ever before and have a whale of a good time doing it.

Do you think tricks are just silly and useless? Read on and surprise yourself.

CAPT. ARTHUR J. HAGGERTY
CAROL LEA BENJAMIN
September 1977

About the Authors

ARTHUR J. HAGGERTY, former commanding officer in the U.S. Army K-9 Corps, is the director of the largest school for theatrical dogs on the east coast of the United States as well as the largest dog school in the world. He is the teacher of hundreds of other dog trainers and his methods of training are being used throughout the world. Trainer par excellence in all aspects of dog work, he is also an award winning author on the subject of dogs. Both Captain Haggerty and the dogs he has trained have appeared in dozens of motion pictures and commercials. His reputation as an innovator in the field of theatrical dogs and trick training is unequalled.

CAROL LEA BENJAMIN, professional dog trainer, award winning author, columnist and cartoonist, is the author of five books about dog behavior and training, among them *DOG TRAINING FOR KIDS* and *DOG PROBLEMS,* both winners of the Dog Writers Association of America Award. Her articles on dogs have appeared in magazines such as *Better Homes and Gardens, Apartment Life, World of the Working Dog* and *Showdogs.* She is the author of a monthly column, Dog Trainer's Diary, for *Pure-bred Dogs, The American Kennel Club Gazette.* Ms. Benjamin appears regularly on radio and television, answering people's questions about their dogs.

1. No Trick Tricks

This easy pair is sweet and simple. The trick to the NO TRICK TRICKS is that *you* are doing the trick rather than your dog. Relax—no experience is necessary.

KISS

Most people who love dogs enjoy getting a kiss on the cheek from an affectionate canine. Even if you say nothing, many dogs will lick your cheek if you present it to them and pet them. If your dog doesn't, or if you want him to do it on command, simply dab a bit of butter on your cheek and say, "Give me a kiss." After a few practice sessions, he will lick your face without the "treat."

If you'd like your dog to look debonair as well as affectionate, try the same technique to get him to kiss a lady's hand. Now make sure he distinguishes the word *cheek* from the word *hand* so that he will deliver exactly the kind of affection you ask him to. He's sure to get many kisses in return and perhaps an occasional blush.

The fundamental things apply . . .

No trick tricks are nearly endless. *Puppy Cordes—German Shepherd*

WAG YOUR TAIL

Several trainers have claimed to originate this trick. But they did not. Neither did we. Whoever invented the dog surely must have included a wagging tail in the original design. So you'll never have to teach your dog to wag his tail. Just talk happily to him and he will. What will you say? You know your dog better than anyone. Just ask him.

Epilogue—No Trick Tricks

We have given only two examples of NO TRICK TRICKS, but in truth they are nearly endless. Watch your dog's behavior and trigger any natural action by naming it when he does it and praising him afterward. He can learn EAT, DRINK, SHAKE, DIG, SCRATCH, STRETCH, YAWN, all with some patience on your part. Get it? We like to give credit where credit is due. The rest is up to you.

2. Retrieving Tricks

Retrieving and tricks go together like ham and eggs. Combined with a few other simple basics, the ability to retrieve will give your dog the foundation for the best of all possible tricks. Furthermore, the discipline of retrieving is great for gaining control over a dog. It helps in all forms of training exercises. However, it is a grueling and strenuous job. It will tax your patience and endurance to the limit. The work will be slow and should be interspersed with your dog's other training. It will take precise timing and diligence plus enough humanity and courage to know when to forge ahead and when to give old Fido a break. If you get through it, you'll both love it. If you give up before your dog does, you'd be better off never beginning. The *taught* method, described below, will work. And *work* is the only "magic" word when it comes to retrieving.

FETCH ON COMMAND

The *taught* method is neither a force method nor a play method. It encompasses some techniques from both these methods plus an understanding of the only hard and fast rule of dog training—that there is no hard and fast rule in dog training. All the answers are not here. If something works, do it. The following principles will serve as a good introduction to the task ahead:

1. All dogs are eager to please—themselves.
2. Play retrieving is great as part of a complete retrieving program.
3. Even a natural retriever has to be made to retrieve sometimes.
4. Your dog must learn to pick up anything he is asked to as long as it is physically possible.
5. Begin retrieving training as early as possible.

6. Progress as rapidly as you can but do not be afraid to go back a step, or even back to square one if necessary.
7. Watch your timing. The key words are COMPULSION; RELEASE FROM COMPULSION; IMMEDIATE REWARD.

Begin to teach retrieving when your dog is undergoing obedience training so that you have some control over him. If he likes chasing balls, let him chase a ball. If he likes chasing sticks, let him chase sticks. Let him get interested in retrieving. Try to get him to bring his prize back to you. Ignore what he has in his mouth. Praise him for *coming* to you. Try his other commands while he is carrying something: HEEL, SIT, STAY, COME. Avoid using the correction NO. It might make him drop the object. If he tries to get you to chase him for the object, move away from him. Pretend not to pay attention to him. When the opportunity is right, he will come to you. Don't make him give you his treasure each time.

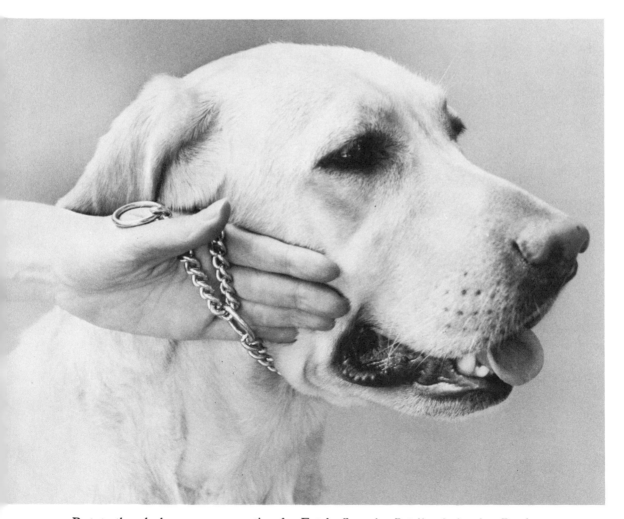

Rotate thumb down as a correction for Fetch. *Sounder Petrik—Labrador Retriever*

Excellent! Now it's time to work with a dowel. An old broom handle will do. Cut off a four- or five-inch piece from the rounded end—or, if you have a toy dog, purchase a thin piece of dowel from the lumberyard. Place the dowel in your right back pocket, rounded side down. With your dog sitting at your side in the Heel position, hold the leash in your left hand. Hold the dowel in your right hand directly in front of the dog's mouth. If your dog turns his head, keep the dowel in front of his mouth. Use the command TAKE IT. The split second he opens his mouth, pop the dowel in and immediately praise your dog. Don't worry if he spits the dowel out. Try again. Speed in praising your dog is extremely important. If he is particularly resistant, put the choke collar high on his neck and slide your hand under it (see illustration, page 5). Your initial purpose in handling the collar in this way is to make sure that the dog is unable to move his head away from the dowel. Firmly and calmly repeat the command TAKE IT. If he does, praise immediately. Now go on to another exercise. Don't badger your dog with retrieving, but keep going back to it. Six of these short sessions will take only two or three minutes. In between, work on obedience or give him a break and let him chase a ball.

Your dog is now taking the dowel and you are ready for a little more compulsion. Dear reader, if this starts to offend you, skip over these passages. Your dog does not *have* to retrieve.

Place the choke collar high on your dog's neck and grasp it tightly with the ring of the collar above your thumb. Close your hand into a fist so that the ring remains on top of the collar and twist the collar in a clockwise fashion. This motion forces your dog's muzzle open and his head forward. Your dog is now reaching for the dowel! Timing is all important. Release the pressure as soon as your dog takes the dowel and *praise him.*

Keep moving the dowel further and further away from your dog. If he takes the dowel and then drops it, don't be concerned. But stop praising him when he drops it. Now your dog is reaching a few inches to grasp the dowel, and you and he are well on your way. Remember that your dog is learning to pick something up from the ground, so begin to move the dowel forward and down. This phase of training is terrific for the waistline.

Variety Is the Spice of Dog Training

Remember that you heard it here—your dog can concentrate for much longer than you think. But, like you, he will lose his concentration if he's bored. Alternate these short exercises with obedience work and play retrieving with his favorite objects. Now you can introduce the dumbbell. It is a bit more cumbersome than the dowel, but it will help your dog learn to pick things up from the ground.

At this point, use the collar "twist" only when your dog balks. When you say TAKE IT, he should gleefully reach forward and down for the dumbbell. He's starting to get hooked on all the physical and verbal praise you give him when he takes the dumbbell. Now if you begin to apply pressure to the collar, he will bolt forward and grasp the dumbbell. Wild horses couldn't keep him from it now. He's no dummy.

Hold the dumbbell near the ground and keep your dog's collar high, but don't keep your hand under it. Placing it high on his neck reminds him that you are ready to make a correction. Now, that reminder will usually suffice. Now try the dumbbell on the floor. It may be hard to believe, but now you're getting somewhere. Wild horses couldn't keep you from your goal. You're no dummy.

Once your dog is picking up the dumbbell from the ground, with fewer and fewer "reminders" from you, let him try it with the dowel—and then with his leash dragging. As you continue to practice, he will become more confident and dependable. This is the right time to make him pick up any article he drops. Just tell him TAKE IT and use the collar if necessary. At this point, getting him to hold an item should be no big trick.

Now introduce the word OUT. On this command, the dog should release the dumbbell easily. If he continues to hold onto it, grasp it with one hand and with your other hand grasp the dog over the muzzle and force him to open his mouth. Repeat the command OUT and praise.

Time for a treat. Your dog will love your next training tool—a box of Cracker Jacks. It's comfortable and lightweight. He'll love the odor and the happy, rattling sound. Have him Heel with the box in his mouth. Now try a rolled-up newspaper or magazine. Wrap masking tape around it first to prevent it from unrolling. Soon your dog will retrieve anything. Pat yourself on the back and give Fido a dog biscuit. Broadway, here you come!

VARIATIONS ON A THEME

You're understandably delighted that old Fido will now retrieve a dowel, dumbbell, or box of Cracker Jacks. Isn't it time to expand his repertoire? How often will you have those items with you when you want him to work? They were chiefly the tools of your trade. Now you can systematically get him to fetch anything by using the same basic methods. What you must remember is that at any hesitation on his part you have to move in rapidly and make a correction. So don't try him on a new item in front of your Aunt Betty. No one wants to see you reprimand your children or correct your dog "in public."

Try your retriever on a pack of cigarettes, scarves of any fabric, key rings in a leather pouch. Progress to plain key rings—he'll have to get used to the taste of metal in his mouth. Be ready to correct him if he balks. You can try quarters, nickels, and then dimes, in that order. Be very careful not to let him swallow a coin, and don't expect him to make change! While he learns to retrieve any object he can manage to pick up, begin to use the names of

He'll love the smell and sound when he's fetching Cracker Jacks. *Oliver Benjamin, C.D.—Golden Retriever*

the objects so that you double the mileage on his education. After all, there is an energy crisis—or at least *we* have one. The work should go faster now that he has the basic skills under his collar, but, like everything else in life, it won't all go smoothly. Patience, persistence, and lots of praise are still required.

FETCH FROM WATER

If you are lucky enough to live near a lake, river, stream, or pond, you can give your dog some marvelous recreation and exercise by having him retrieve from water. If he has already swum the English Channel, you can begin by throwing a stick a few feet out and encouraging him to swim to it, fetch it, and bring it back to you. Be prepared to get soaked, because he's sure to do his shaking as close to you as possible.

If Fido has never gotten his feet wet, the easiest way to make a swimmer out of him is to get your own paws into the drink. Find a spot where it's safe and legal, wait for a balmy day, and go for a swim. He won't need much encouragement to join you. He just won't want to be left behind on the shore. Call to him and swim around. Call to him and swim away. Try not to let him swim too close to you while he's still a nervous beginner. He might scratch you. Encourage, praise, enjoy. Now that he's ready for the Olympic Swimming Team, you can have him retrieve sticks from the water with no trouble at all.

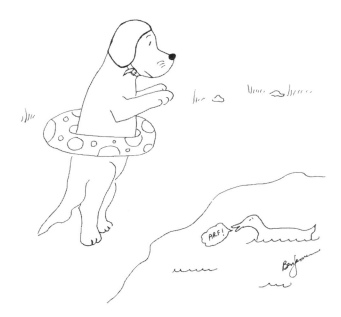

First, teach him to swim.

3. Scent Discrimination Tricks

The dog's skills for scent discrimination rank high among his most astounding talents because man, no matter how intelligent, simply cannot duplicate these feats. Furthermore, humans are only at the beginning of an understanding of how dogs function in tracking and scent discrimination. Using your dog's scenting abilities will not only give you satisfaction: your dog will be thrilled to exercise and expand these unique talents. In this case, your praises will only serve as fringe benefits for Fido, but you'll be inspired to lavish them anyway. Try it and see.

SMELL IT—FIND IT!

The initial motivation for this trick is built into its first step. Begin with a dog biscuit or small morsel of dry dog food. With your dog on a Sit Stay, hold the food up to his nose and tell him to smell it. If he grabs for it, tell him NO. The hand, in this case, must be quicker than the mouth. Again, tell him to smell it. When you see his nostrils move, praise him and take the food away. Drop or place the food a few feet away from him where he can still see it. Now tell him OKAY, FIND IT! The OKAY will break the Sit Stay and he will go right for the food and eat it. Now you can praise him quite enthusiastically. Practice this step until he neither grabs for the food nor breaks to find and eat it.

Begin to place the biscuit farther and farther away. By now your dog is on to the "game" and enjoys it immensely because he gets the double reward of food and praise when he finds the biscuit. Now he is ready to find the biscuit when you hide it out of sight. Let him watch you carry it into the next room. Place it in an obvious spot on the floor so that he will have no difficulty in spotting it right away. In this way, he will succeed every time and build his confidence in finding things. Be sure you never let him slip—that is, don't

A built-in motivation—food! *Maggie Maresco—Poodle Mix*

let him take the food when sniffing it or break his Stay before you command. Now hide the food on a slight elevation such as the first step on a flight of steps or the bottom shelf of a bookcase. Praise him warmly when he finds it. Continue very slowly to make the hunt more difficult, placing the biscuit higher or perhaps between two books on the shelf. Encourage him as he works.

Now go from room to room and let him find out which room the treat is hidden in as part of his search. If ever he has great trouble, you have probably gone too fast for him, so slow up the training by giving him more practice with easy finds. If he is swift in his work and enthusiastic, you may try hiding the biscuit behind the drapes or in your pocket.

FIND THE BALL

Your dog will love playing SMELL IT—FIND IT! because he will love the opportunity to use his specialized scenting abilities. That trick, and this variation of it, adapts well if you are a multiple dog owner. All your dogs can play at once. The dog who finds the object wins the round. No need to keep score. The dogs couldn't care less. Their fun is in the game.

Now you can play SMELL IT—FIND IT! with a ball. To play properly, you will have taught your dog to retrieve. This way, when he finds the ball, he will fetch it and bring it back to you for his praise. In fact, you can send him to find the hidden ball while you wait in another room for him to bring it back to you. He'll get a kick out of working independently.

Begin by letting your dog smell the ball. Tell him to STAY and proceed slowly as in the previous trick. Once he has made increasingly difficult finds with exuberant praise from you, begin to have him TAKE IT and back up, calling him to come all the way to where the game began. Thus he will learn to make a find, retrieve it, and return it to you. Again, use obvious hiding places and slowly progress to more difficult ones. The point is not to outwit your dog but to teach him, step by step, to always succeed.

This game is a grand way to teach your dog some new words. One at a time, have him find a ball, a glove, a box of Cracker Jacks, an eyeglass case, etc. Then begin to line up two or three things and ask him to find and bring them to you one at a time, *by name*. This will all be facilitated by your prior work on having him retrieve all these objects. Ready? Play ball!

FIND A PERSON

If you own a Bloodhound, live near a state penitentiary, and have a flair for drama, don't read this trick. Go out and get yourself a serious book on tracking. We cannot possibly teach you here everything you've always wanted to know about tracking. For our purposes, the dog's exciting skills as a tracker will be put to lighter use. It's fun, and if you'll pardon the pun, safer by a long shot than chasing criminals.

Your terrific dog can find people by trial and error (not a bad trick) or by using his tracking or scenting skills (a great trick). You can tell Perry Mason to go find your son Tom. He's heard Tom's name hundreds of times. He may poke around the house trying to figure out what you want. Point him in the right direction. And clue Tom in to his role. Play it like the kids play Hot or Cold, encouraging him along verbally. When he stumbles accidentally upon your son, both of you should praise him wildly. Try it a few more times, and then switch roles.

If you want your dog to do some fancier nose work, take him out to a field. Have your son walk twenty feet away, but still in sight. Send Perry to find Tom. Keep him on leash (No, not your son! Your dog!), let him pull you,

If he holds his head up and sniffs the wind, he is scouting.

and have Tom ready to receive him with open arms and lots of praise. Gradually make the search harder until Tom hides out of sight.

Your dog may actually track your son or he may find him by scouting (winding). If he is tracking, his nose will be to the ground and he will be following ground scent. If he holds his head up and sniffs the wind, he is using the natural and speedy method of scouting to locate his missing person. The scent he will seek comes from the person in a cone shape, getting wider as it diffuses. The farther away Perry is from Tom, the wider and less concentrated the scent. As he works on more difficult finds, he may not lead you directly in. He may go from side to side as he moves forward, or, depending upon the direction of the wind, he may work up one side of the cone. As the scent gets stronger, he will move more rapidly. It all depends on how he works the scent cone. Trust him. Even if you have a nose like Jimmy Durante, you won't know where the scent is strongest.

Back to the field and your son, who is by now tired and hungry. Give it one more try. Tell Perry FIND IT, FIND IT and be prepared to move fast. This trick, if you give it the time and a variety of missing persons, will teach you more about dogs and their special skills than almost any other. If you want to keep it light, stay indoors and send Perry for praise to any member of your household. He'll love the attention, the change of pace, and a legitimate chance to sniff.

CARRY A MESSAGE

This is a useful trick for even the smallest household—as long as there are at least two of you. Your message doesn't have to be a love letter, though we advocate you give that at least one try. Carrying a message can mean, "Bring Mother her glasses," or "Here's the checkbook—you owe me ten," and, right! "Here's the pen to sign it with." Unless your dog is rare indeed, don't send anyone a Swiss cheese sandwich. But as long as your dog is a good retriever, why not put him to work? Will he feel exploited? Not in the least! He'll be helping you and getting a big kick out of what to him is just a terrific game.

You have done your groundwork with retrieving and now it's time to play. Garcia, your trick dog, will enjoy impressing you and your company with his antics. Start off at a short distance from one of your six kids. Children adore this trick. Command Garcia BRING IT, BRING IT TO BABETTE and have Babette call your dog. Place your emphasis on your child's name. It is important that the message gets to the right person— especially if it *is* a love letter. Garcia will trot right over to Babette amid admiring sighs and pats—the perfect reward for your enthusiastic mail dog. Now Babette can tell Garcia DADDY, BRING IT TO DADDY! Have her send back a different item. You don't want your dog rushing all over the house with the one item you started him on. Extend the distance between you until you are in different rooms. Take five. And now work with one of your five other kids; you don't want the dog to carry *everything* to Babette. He must learn to listen to the name in the command.

Think of the practical applications of this trick! The farmer working in the field can send the dog in for his sun hat. Perhaps your dog will bring your mittens when you are shoveling the driveway. If you're in a four-flight walkup, you can send your child a shopping list and money without braving all those steps—provided Garcia doesn't get mugged in the hallway! And what a way to send someone a special note. The things we do for love!

Whenever possible, think romantic!

4. Oldies but Goodies

The following are the best of the classics. No, of course *we* didn't make them up—we're not *that* old. But while they may be old hat to some, try telling an audience that your fabulous trick dog doesn't give his paw or roll over and play dead. You'll be surprised and delighted with the mileage left on these old beauties—some "untouched" and some with a fresh, new twist. Don't skip them—trust us.

GIVE YOUR PAW

Everyone knows how to do this trick. Say GIVE YOUR PAW and pick up Harpo's paw. Repeat this over and over again. You can reduce the number of repetitions if you stay attuned to your dog. A dog will lift its paw on a number of occasions without knowing this exercise. He will paw you if he wants attention, wants to be petted or scratched. So do it—pet him and scratch him—*after* you say GIVE YOUR PAW. Most dogs will give their left paw. The majority of people are "righties" and reach for the closest paw. What a plot for a mystery—Supersleuth finds a dog left at the scene of the crime. When he says GIVE YOUR PAW, the dog lifts his right paw. "Aha! The criminal is left-handed."

This simple fact lets you jazz up this nice old trick. Tell Harpo GIVE ME THE OTHER PAW. Good old dog, craving attention, will try the other paw to gain it. Grasp it, praise him, tell him he's wonderful, and you're off to the races.

Your dog will also extend his paw when he assumes a submissive posture because he has done something wrong. This is a first step in the dog's behavior pattern of submission, to be followed ultimately by his rolling over. When his paw comes up, give the command, take the paw, and reassure him. Do not use this technique if your dog has done something awful on your Persian rug. When he has given you one paw, firmly say NO, THE OTHER PAW. He will submissively offer the other paw. Take it and praise him. Now you can build this exercise into RIGHT PAW, LEFT PAW. But you can show off even before your dog learns it well. Your patter, "No, not that paw, the right paw, now the other paw, the left paw, no, the other paw," can be more effective than actually doing RIGHT PAW, LEFT PAW.

PLAY DEAD

This ordinary trick will go into orbit with the right twist. For this old standard, your dog should remain motionless as he lies on his side. He is steadier and less likely to move lying on his side than lying on his stomach. Of course, your dog already knows the down command. Tell him DOWN and note which side he is leaning toward. Get down near him on that side and gently push on his shoulder to roll him over onto his side. In a calm voice, give the command BANG! (Yes—BANG! Patience, dear friends.) As Rollo rolls over onto his side, pet him and give his tummy a little scratch. If he starts to roll all the way over onto his back, gently bring him back to his side, petting his shoulder as you do. The best time to work on this trick is after Rollo has had some strenuous exercise and is ready for a rest. Gradually lengthen the time he will play dead, and don't work on this trick when he is in a wild or active mood.

Now that Rollo is beginning to respond well, point your finger at him and say BANG! Aha! He will drop to the floor, shot down in the prime of life, and roll over to his side, where he will remain limp and motionless until you

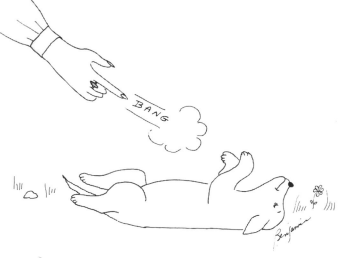

Shot down in the prime of life.

release him with your enthusiastic praise. If you're really a patient soul, you can expand upon this trick so that Rollo becomes totally limp when playing dead. Tranquilize him: hypnotize him with your voice and gentle, soothing manner. If you give it the time, you will be able to lift his tail or a leg and let it fall to the ground like dead weight. No need to explain the meaning of death to your little actor. Caress him, soothe him with your voice, gradually lift his foreleg and let it drop. Put your fingers over his eyes and make him blink so that he closes them. All the while, softly tell him BANG, PLAY DEAD. Think of the fun your kids will have "bringing him back to life."

ROLL OVER

ROLL OVER is taught from the DEAD DOG position. It is taught when you and Rollo are in a happy, up mood. Work at playtime for best results. Rollo will move in the direction opposite to the way his legs are pointed. While he can be taught to roll one way all the time, it looks much better if he can roll either way. Therefore, he must be taught to PLAY DEAD with his legs facing either way.

Rollo is playing dead. Grasp the "off side" legs and rapidly but carefully flip him over, saying ROLL OVER. As Rollo rolls over, let him get up right away. And you jump up and play with him. He doesn't have to stay in the down position, but make sure that he rolls over completely and doesn't just jump up. As you work, teach him the hand signal by moving your right hand in a circular motion *in the direction he is to travel.* In this way, by hand signal alone, you will be able to have him roll over in one direction and then the other—an accomplishment in anyone's book.

As Rollo catches on and begins to enjoy this trick, work from farther and farther away. You'll find this good practice if you do break into show biz with Rollo. No one will want you right on top of the cameramen—so you will have to direct your star from a distance, silently. If Rollo is reluctant—out of sight, out of mind—work with his leash on him. The leash is drawn from the collar and then placed under his outstretched lower forequarter. Say ROLL OVER and exert an upward pressure on the leash. As he rolls over, release the pressure so that his legs don't get tangled in the leash. If you are heavy-handed with this correction, you might cause your dog to take a spill. So work carefully.

Now you can Heel with Rollo. As you stroll along, point your finger at Rollo—BANG! Now circle your hand and he rolls over, several times if you prefer. Tap your leg, he's back at Heel. Try it again—and again. Now get a clown suit and you're in business.

SIT HIGH (BEG)

More dogs teach themselves this trick than any other one, and their owners humbly take the credit. That's fine. Your dog couldn't care less.

In this trick, as in life, position is everything. Your dog must learn to sit squarely on both hindquarters. As you build a house from the foundation up, this trick is built from the hindquarters up. Though some dogs try to do this and even succeed with a bent spine, this is undesirable and will cause the dog to give up rather quickly.

How does one get a dog to SIT HIGH if he does not do it naturally? You must learn an expert touch in handling the leash. The pressure should not be so great as to make the dog gag, yet it must not be so light that he will fall over or come down from the SIT HIGH position. Timing and touch will be all important. What you are aiming for is to teach the dog to adjust his body so that the hindquarters are square, the weight of the thorax is over the hindquarters, and the forequarters are folded into the chest to prevent unbalancing himself. When viewing the dog from the side, his back should be straight. It should not form an "S" and he should bear no resemblance to the Leaning Tower of Pisa. He should not be allowed to reach forward with his paws for imagined support. This would shift his weight forward and throw him off balance.

More dogs teach themselves this trick than any other.

There are a couple of crutches you can use in teaching this exercise. You can put your dog into a corner and gradually lift him up with the leash attached to his choke collar. With his back to the wall, he'll have a sense of security. And so will you. At least you'll know he won't spill over backwards. Another crutch is preferred, as it allows you to do the exercise anywhere, not only in a corner of your house. The dog will get the same back support from you. With your dog sitting, stand directly behind him, in Charlie Chaplin fashion. Your feet, heels together, toes pointing out, will be running

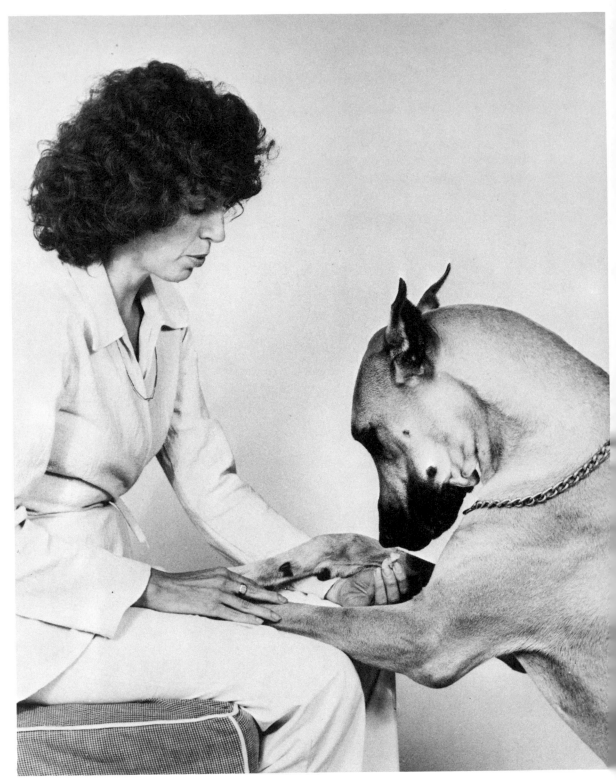

A morsel of food held between her forelegs will get her to bend her head. *Butz McGuire—Great Dane*

alongside his hindquarters. His back will be supported by your legs. You are now directly over the dog and can easily pick up the leash. There are no walls to cramp your style and the dog feels secure against your legs. You are in an ideal position to tuck his paws into his chest and caress him for doing a good job.

With any of the above techniques, the correct results depend upon the positioning of the hindquarters, thorax, forequarters, and even the dog's head. This, plus a judicious on and off leash pressure, will steady the dog as you draw him upward. Once he seems to be getting the idea and learning the new command, try baiting him with a tidbit of cheese to get him to SIT HIGH. Now you can increase the time he stays in the SIT HIGH position by talking to him and making him wait for his treat.

SAY YOUR PRAYERS

Hidden in this old goody are some commands you will use when teaching other tricks as well. When you tell Mimi to say her prayers, she will put her front paws up on whatever you indicate and drop her head reverently between them. While you speak some appropriate words, she will remain solemnly in position. When you say AMEN, she will break.

Begin by teaching your dog PAWS UP. This can be easily done either on a counter, the side of your bed, or even on your lap. Mimi should pray from a sitting position if the surface is low and a standing position if it is a high counter. Tap your legs and tell Mimi PAWS UP. If she's reluctant (no doubt you've taught her *not* to jump on people, so you will have to break this inhibition on command only), offer a treat that she can get only by placing her paws up on your lap. Make sure she remains sitting, praise her, and tell her STAY. Now, telling her HIDE YOUR EYES, hold the treat between her forequarters and below them so that she has to dip her head down to get it (see illustration). Begin repeating SAY YOUR PRAYERS, holding the treat for a moment so that she cannot eat it. Now, as you say AMEN, GOOD GIRL, let her have the treat and break. Repeat this procedure a few times in each session.

As Mimi begins to learn each step, reduce your commands so that you just have to say SAY YOUR PRAYERS and AMEN. Now you can play with the trick. Your prayer (or hers, if you prefer) will be limited only by your sense of humor. She can pray for lunch, for a handsome boy dog, for a walk, for a raise in salary for her master. Practice Mimi's "prayers" on the edge of your bed or wherever you tell her to say them. Gradually build her patience so that you can fool around with longer and longer prayers. It'll be a very impressive skill if one day you and Mimi have an audience with the Pope.

BALANCE AND CATCH

This popular trick is fairly simple, yet it is nonetheless flashy. BALANCE AND CATCH is based on previous exercises that you have taught your dog. The commands are SIT HIGH, STAY, and OKAY. While STAY and OKAY are not covered in this book, they are part of the obedience foundation your dog has been taught before beginning any trick training.

Muffin sits high and you place a small piece of cookie, cheese, or dog biscuit on her nose. Steady her by holding her muzzle. You do not want the biscuit to roll off. Now your dog's mouth is already watering, so we will proceed rapidly. As you say OKAY, she will snap her head to toss and catch the biscuit. The first time she tries, she may send it sailing across the room. If so, she will sail across the room in pursuit of her goody. That's fine. This will be her motivation until she learns how to catch it. Let her enjoy her treat and then position her again. Steady her, telling her STA-AY. Hold her muzzle for a moment with your thumb and middle finger while your index finger steadies the biscuit. Now, in a reassuring, drawn-out voice, tell her OKAAY. She must be slowed down in order to have enough control to catch the biscuit. If she is too wild and excited, she won't balance the biscuit or she'll continue to send it across the room at jet-propelled speeds. As you slow her down, she will begin to make successful catches.

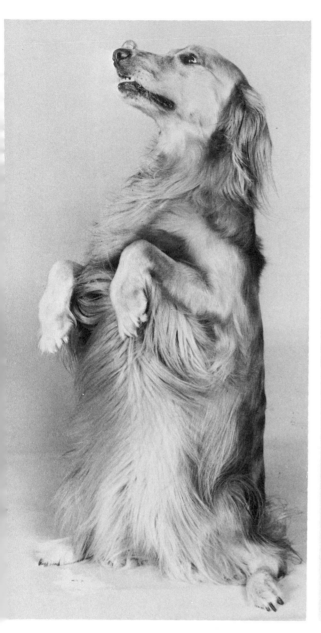 

STAAAAY.   OKAY! *Muffin Haggerty—Golden Retriever*

Make sure that you use the same size tidbits and place them on the same spot on Muffin's nose to facilitate her learning. Changing spots and sizes will make her work much more difficult. Most dogs will have the best luck with the tidbit immediately behind the nose. But you will have to experiment slightly to find the best spot for your Muffin.

The rather easy trick shows up well because it implies great control on the part of your dog and an especially nice rapport between you and your canine pal. It is also a swell way to keep your dog's education going when you are in the mood to give a treat.

BRING THE NEWSPAPER

This classic trick can be of great service to dog owners. It can save needless steps or be a great comfort when the weather is chilly or terribly hot. While you are happily relaxing, your dog will be happily working. Don't forget—he's unemployed and always looking for something to do.

You have taught your dog to retrieve and have practiced him on various items of different textures. Now take a section of the Sunday paper, roll it tightly, and tape it with masking tape so that it can't unroll. Toss it for your dog, saying TAKE IT, BRING THE PAPER. If you've done a good job, so will he. Praise him and repeat this a few times a day whenever you are in the mood.

Now begin to let him bring your dummy paper from outside. Toss it to wherever your paper boy leaves your paper—just outside your door, on the edge of the driveway, in the bushes. If it's usually on the roof, forget this trick and don't tip the paper boy! Once your dog will get the paper from its usual spot, practice having him pick up the folded paper—unless yours is delivered in a plastic bag or rolled and rubber banded (in which case your dummy should be likewise). Now when you hear that familiar thud, simply open your front door and ask Arfie to BRING THE PAPER. Naturally, if he's a runaway and your yard isn't fenced, you'll work on his off-leash training first! If not, you'll have no help with the crossword puzzle.

WALK ON HIND LEGS

This is an important trick for a well-rounded repertoire. Small dogs are often naturals at this trick because they are always trying to get up higher to see what is happening around them. You can encourage such a dog by holding tidbits over his head and rewarding him for walking. Of course, because of the strength you would need to be able to teach this trick to a huge dog, this cannot be considered a trick for every dog. Fifi the Toy Poodle will learn this rapidly, but Sean the Irish Wolfhound will have to find his kicks elsewhere.

Check SIT HIGH for a description of the proper positioning of the hips, thorax, forelegs, and head. The same applies to walking on the hind legs. If your dog falls into the natural category, she will properly position herself. If not, it will be part of your job.

Put a flat leather collar on Fifi and attach a standard leash. With a tidbit in your right hand and the leash in your left, pull directly upward and command WALK. Be sure to ball up the excess leash into your hand to keep it out of Fifi's eyes. Remember to line up all the parts of Fifi's body. You may feel a forward motion with Fifi reaching out in front of herself with her forequarters. Initially, let her do this, but shortly you will want to teach her to keep her paws tucked into her body. Reaching forward will throw her off balance and she will move her body forward to try to regain it. Though we want a forward motion, it is more important at this stage for Fifi to learn how to keep her balance. Begin the command STAND . . . HIGH. The pause will give her time to get into position. As she gets better and faster, shorten the command to STAND HIGH.

If your dog is not a natural, work very short sessions. The collar will cause some discomfort, and you do not want to hurt your dog. She will also need time to build the strength to do this trick for longer periods of time. Watch your leash timing carefully. *As soon as her position is good, you must slack off on the leash.* This is an immediate reward for Fifi. The method is repeated compulsion (pulling up on the leash) and release from compulsion (loosening the leash the split second her position is correct) with a food reward at the end of each set. Compulsion is not introduced unless Fifi starts to get out of position by letting her forequarters move downward. Whenever she stays up for a reasonable period of time, give her a food reward. A delicate timing and an ability to relate to your dog's feelings are critical in this exercise.

Once your dog is up on her hindquarters, you can move the food to get her to walk, or *slowly* move the leash forward, saying WALK. When you can move her forward, then try a circle. Now you can hire a band and Fifi will dance.

Hire a band and Fifi will dance. *Melissa Zaretsky—Schnoodle*

5. Silly Tricks

Do silly tricks have a place in your dog's repertoire? Indeed they do. They are valuable primarily because they can make people laugh and feel good. While it is wrong to laugh *at* a dog's mistakes or at his "cute" disobedience, it is fine to laugh with him. He feels your pleasure and responds to your light and cheery attitude. He loves to share any kind of enjoyment with you.

Silly tricks have a serious purpose too. The teaching of anything to your dog, done fairly and clearly, will help your communication with him and increase his ability to learn and be attentive. So if you're a good time Charlie, why not include your dog in the act?

CARRY A PIPE

This bit of fluff will make children and immature adults laugh and feel silly. It can be great, too, for a gag photo for homemade personal greeting cards. Buy Herm a small, light pipe. Don't offend his sensibilities with a used pipe. Now put Herm on a Sit Stay. Offer him a "smoke," telling him TAKE IT. Place the stem of the pipe in his mouth, reminding him TAKE IT, HOLD IT. Try this one or two times a session for a couple of days. Now load your camera, give Herm his pipe and shoot. Trick done, put your feet up, and rest.

WEAR A HAT, SCARF, TIE

It wouldn't be fair to leave this charming nonsense out of a trick book. Perhaps we'll weigh down our fluff with a serious point. If you have done your preliminary work properly, your dog will wear a chicken suit if it

Dressed to the teeth, she can observe the passing parade. *Bosco Halboth—Shepherd Mix*

pleases you. And if you haven't, don't waste your money on that double-breasted, back-belted mink jacket you've ordered for her. Let this silly trick test your relationship with your dog. All you need to make Coco wear anything is good control over her. When sedately on a Sit Stay, if it tickles your fancy (or your children's), she can wear a scarf, a tie, a hat with a ribbon or string. She can wear a T-shirt that says, "Kiss me, I'm Irish," or little rain boots in the winter. So have a good time and take some great photos. (Please send us the best ones for our next book.) And while you're at it, see if Coco is amenable to your whimsy. If she isn't, with slight encouragement, work a little harder on her obedience lessons.

While you're working on any trick, never lose the opportunity to teach Coco more English. At the same time, you'll be improving the trick. Ask her to get her hat and bring it to you. Then you can be a gentleman and help her on with it. How on earth can you get her to do that? Don't be a politician. Don't toss your hat in the ring—throw hers across the room. Tell her TAKE IT, TAKE YOUR HAT. Once she knows what you mean by "hat," keep it in one spot she can reach. Now—OK, COCO. TIME TO GO OUT. GET YOUR HAT.

If so inclined, you can have an outfit made to order.

PUSH A CARRIAGE

If you want a dog that will dress up in silly clothes, this trick is about as ridiculous as you can get. Yet, for some strange reason, when part of a polished circus act, this one steals the show. So, while dressing up dogs isn't our bag, if it's yours, we won't argue with you. We won't even tell!

Picking the perfect perambulator is not that difficult. Consideration should be given to the size of the dog and the size of the baby carriage. If your dog is rather small, choose from the wide selection of doll baby carriages. If Amelda already knows how to walk on her hindquarters, this trick will be that much easier. Even if she does not have the energy to walk on her hindquarters for a long period of time, she can do it pushing a pram. She will be able to rest and distribute her weight on the handle of the carriage. If necessary, weigh down the carriage to keep it from tipping over as she shifts her weight to the handle.

Begin with a broom handle and tell Amelda PAWS UP as you hold the broom directly in front of her. Adjust the height of the broom handle to the approximate height of the baby carriage. You will do this even if Amelda knows how to walk on her hindquarters. Face Amelda and walk backward as you tell her FORWARD. Do not let her put her whole weight on the broom handle. Elevate it so that the bulk of her weight is placed on her hindquarters. Play with the height and angle of the broom handle until you have Amelda exerting a forward, pushing motion. This becomes a technique similar to that of playing a fish on a line. It requires an understanding and feel for your dog. As soon as Amelda gets the idea, introduce the baby carriage and now you can walk alongside of her. Encourage her with the command FORWARD and give her a lot of verbal praise. Be sure to be ready to catch the carriage if it should start to tip over! You can keep one hand under the handle for just such an emergency. If both dog and pram fall to the ground, Amelda may not want to walk her baby again and you'll have a difficult time encouraging her back to work.

If you are going to do this trick, do it right. One dog is good. You can put a doll in the carriage. Two dogs are better. One, in a dress, pushes the carriage. The other, Baby, wears a bonnet and rides. Sillier than this we can't get!

SINGING

There are innumerable shaggy dog stories about singing and talking dogs. Everyone has heard about these eloquent animals and doggy divas, but few have seen them in the "fur." However, with the right dog, singing is actually an easy trick—as well as immensely charming. But you might not have the right dog. Generally, sled dogs have a propensity for singing arias. Hit a high-pitched sound, the head goes up, muzzle at a forty-five-degree angle, and they howl as long as the sound continues. Fire engines, as you well know if you own a "northern breed," are great for starting these dogs off. Please don't set your house on fire or rush out and buy a fire engine. You don't even have to rush out and buy a Siberian Husky. If your dog isn't a natural singer, you can still accomplish this trick.

The only hard part of this trick is finding the high-pitched sound that will trigger your Caruso and make him break into song. Try the following for starters: a touch-tone phone, a soprano recorder, a tape recording of a siren, high notes on your piano, a harmonica, a sweet potato (no, not the baked kind). A visit to the local music store with your trained dog will save several unnecessary purchases. Just buy the instrument that works and hope it's not the grand piano. Last, but not least, try your own voice. If you sing as we do, your dog is the only one who'll listen to you anyway. Hitting the highest note you can may do it. If your dog reacts by putting his paws over his ears, forget singing—you have just invented a better trick.

6. Parlor Tricks

Everyone likes to put on the dog for company—but now you can do it literally. Who knows? These fun exercises may even replace dessert. Your guests will enjoy watching your pooch go through his paces. What a swell way to say, "Love me. Love my dog!"

TAKE FOOD FROM MY MOUTH

This trick could well qualify as a silly trick. Surely it will win you and Oliver some silly giggles. But it has a serious purpose behind it, as do so many of the other tricks in this book. A dog who grabs food is a dangerous dog. In his exuberance to chow down, he may accidentally bite the hand that feeds him. If he's greedy and rude, he may even bite by design. Some of what he covets may not be intended for him at all. If you're in the habit of gesturing with a bread stick or half of a tuna sandwich, in one fell swoop you may lose your food and your fingers.

Your first step, then, is the serious job of teaching your dog not to take any food without the release word OKAY. This won't entirely prevent him from being a chicken thief—especially if you leave your bird on the table to cool (or defrost) when you go out to the movies. But it surely will inhibit him from stealing and will make him take food more gently when he takes it from your hand—or mouth.

As early as possible, begin to tell your puppy OKAY when he is receiving food. Once in a while, hold up some food and say NO. If your puppy tries to take the food, don't let him, saying NO again. If he waits, say OKAY and give him the food. Then praise him. After a little practice, your puppy or dog should not even go to his dinner bowl until he hears you say OKAY. Now you are ready for this trick.

Begin with a large-sized dog biscuit (or a bread stick if you are fussy about holding a dog biscuit in your mouth). Hold the biscuit in your teeth so that most of it sticks out of your mouth. Have your dog on a Sit Stay so that he is under control. Kneel down next to him, let him sniff the biscuit, and say OKAY. If he is gentle, slowly proceed to smaller biscuits. If he grabs, go back and work with him on taking food gently on command before you proceed.

For sound effects, try the trick with a large potato chip. As he bites, *crunch,* you'll each get half. You can do the same thing with a bread stick by biting down, as he does, instead of releasing the stick. One dog we know got so into the trick that he picked up his dusty old bone from under the bed and offered it to his owner to take in her mouth. Being a true dog lover and not wanting to disappoint her old buddy, she did. Some people will go to any lengths to please a dog.

Where Angels Fear to Tread

If your little angel takes well to this trick, you can really get daring. Take a strand of cooked spaghetti, with or without sauce, and dangle it from your mouth. Tell him OKAY, TAKE IT. If he coaxes the spaghetti from your lips, try shorter and shorter strands to wow your guests and send them into fits of belly laughter. If you make it to pastina, give us a call.

CARRY A BASKET AND SERVE FOOD

This is one of the cutest tricks you could possibly imagine and worth every second of the work it takes to teach it to your dog. Friends come for dinner and socialize over drinks beforehand. Suddenly, who should appear from the kitchen but Garçon, your dog. In his mouth he holds a basket with assorted nuts and he glides confidently among your guests offering them these treats to go with their drinks. After dinner, he can bring cookies to go with the coffee or after-dinner mints, if you prefer. Incredible? We're terrific? We knew you'd see it our way. Roll up your sleeves and let's get to it.

Purchasing the right prop will make all the difference. So will going back to Fetch on Command (in Chapter 2) and teaching your dog to retrieve. Find a basket that your dog can carry. If it hits him in the chest or won't hang straight, it will be too clumsy. If he's well trained, take him with you to the store. It will save buying and bringing home a dozen baskets for him to try.

Begin Garçon with an empty basket. Tell him TAKE IT, HOLD IT, THAT'S A GOOD BOY, HOLD IT. If he drops it, have him pick it up. Help him to find a comfortable position by placing the handle behind his eyeteeth. Now get Garçon to Heel with the basket in his mouth. Just work with him a few minutes a day so that he gradually gets used to carrying the basket—and praise him warmly when he does. Now you can have your family sit around in the living room, with or without cocktails. Tell Garçon to go to each of them in turn, carrying his little basket (see Find a Person, in Chapter 3). Let them pretend to take something out of the basket and praise him enthusiastically. All the attention will convince Garçon of the wisdom of his new job.

Now you can fill the basket, halfway, with cookies or peanuts. If you like, or if you have fuss budgety friends, toss a linen napkin over the top to keep the food clean. Or use a covered small picnic basket. After all, your dog's no machine and he may drool a bit. Again, tell Garçon GO TO BETTE, GO TO ARTHUR, GO TO BABETTE, GO TO VICKI and have him wait while they help themselves to some food. Have him return to you last for some extra praise and a treat. It's better, of course, if the treat is one of *his*

Announce that your dog accepts tips!

snacks, or else you may find him sneaking off into a corner to demolish a whole basket of peanuts at your next cocktail party. Finally, Garçon is ready for his debut. If it's just going to be your brother-in-law, we wish you luck. However, if it's going to be a grand party, invite us. We adore parties and we're in the Yellow Pages!

Now that your dog is serving food, you can announce that he does indeed accept tips—and proceed as follows:

Retrieving Coins: A Refresher Course for Greedy Dog Owners

If you'll check back to Variations on a Theme in Chapter 2, you'll find that you were asked to have your dog retrieve quarters, nickels, and dimes. You probably had a good laugh and went on to the next trick. But watching a dog retrieve a coin is exciting and you can probably use the extra change. Try a large coin. If Garçon balks, try him on a wooden checker and work him down to a tiddlywink. If he's retrieving on command, he can and will pick up coins. The smaller the object, the faster *you* should retrieve it from him. Given time to play with it, he may decide to swallow it. If he does, don't panic—but do call your vet. If he doesn't swallow it, have your piggy bank ready.

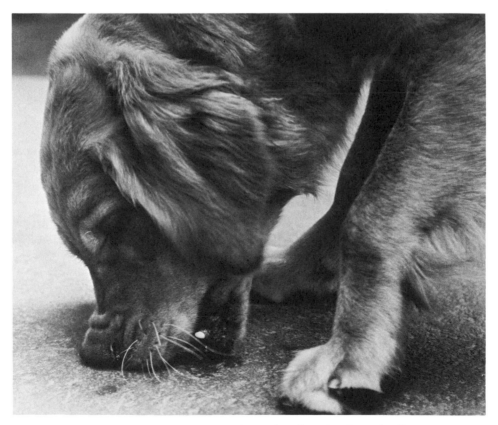

She'll scoop up the dimes and you can have the piggy bank ready. *Fanny Benjamin —Golden Retriever*

BRING A CHAIR

This is an exercise that separates the dogs from the puppies! You'll need one enormous dog and one chair. Moose will have to be a reliable retriever —and he will truly have to be a moose! The best type of dog for this job is the one that is always carrying huge things around the yard. If your moose grabs large tree limbs and tries to carry them through narrow doorways or if he uses a car tire as a teething ring, you have an excellent candidate for this trick. Some dogs enjoy carrying car tires. The tires make inexpensive toys that Moose won't wear out overnight. After all, they took you over 27,000 miles first. With this kind of dog, a tough trick like Bring a Chair becomes a possibility. However, if a slender Saluki is more to your liking, relax on the chair and send him to fetch your ivory cigarette holder. There are no miracles in this book.

You will have to find the balancing point on the chair you choose, and mark it off with masking tape. The balancing point is the point at which the chair can be elevated and carried without tipping or dragging on the floor. And this must work from your dog's height. Start off with an old aluminum lawn chair. Don't use a new one—it may take quite a beating. The aluminum chair, though light in weight, will get Moose used to the bulkiness of a chair. If Moose is the kind of dog described above, you will be able to build up the weight he will have to carry very rapidly.

Guide Moose to the taped balancing point of the chair and tell him TAKE IT. Place the taped part of the chair in his mouth and praise him. Now encourage him to take a few steps with the chair in his mouth. Stay close to him so that you can prevent him from dropping the chair on his own toes. Work for a few minutes every day and gradually increase the distance that Moose is willing to carry the chair. This is good practice work, but a wooden chair makes a much more impressive tool for this trick. Find a light one, perhaps a child's chair, and tape the balancing point. You can build Moose's ability to carry heavier chairs systematically the way a weight lifter increases the weight he can lift. Always stay near Moose to prevent him from dropping the chair and hurting himself. Once he has mastered an adult-sized wooden chair, you can start letting him move on his own for a few steps. You and Moose will have to work very hard, but the results will be remarkable indeed.

Now Moose is ready for action. The next time you have a houseguest, turn to Moose and say MOOSE, BRING A CHAIR. He will trot out and return with his "marked" chair in his mouth. Be ready to take it from him quickly before your guest passes out!

CATCH IT—PLAY BALL

Begin with your dog on a Sit Stay. Use a small dog biscuit, let him smell it, and back up a few feet. His eye will be on your hand that is holding the biscuit. So far, so good. Tell him, CATCH IT, and toss the biscuit to him, aiming about at his nose. It's the right spot for him to make a good catch and will make a nice bull's-eye for you to aim at. Don't try to make it tough on him. You *want* him to catch it. If he sits there looking dimwitted and lets the biscuit bounce off his head, never fear. It's a normal first reaction. It may even take him a few days to make his first catch. Let him break and eat your toss, whether he catches it or not, until he is a successful catcher fifty per cent of the time. This will get him sold on the trick.

Once he is making a decent try and his batting average is worth bragging about, don't let him eat the biscuit *unless he catches it.* If he misses and begins to get up, tell him NO, STAY and toss another, saying CATCH IT. Then you can pick up his misses and toss those again. A few minutes a day will be plenty of practice on this trick unless you want an obese dog. Dog biscuits are nutritious but high in calories. So when teaching this trick, cut down on his regular chow a bit.

Once your biscuit catcher is hooked on this game, switch him to a tennis ball. (If he's a toy breed, a jacks ball will do.) By now he enjoys catching and won't mind an inedible toss. If he's reluctant, switch off between the food and the ball for a while. If you're as lazy as we are, once he catches the ball call him to come. Say OUT (see Fetch on Command), take the ball, and send him out for another catch. Without any fancy training, if you make a false throw he should be on his way. Tell him SIT and then CATCH IT. Son of a gun, you've done it again.

This trick could save your dog's life! *Foxy Donaldson—Pembroke Welsh Corgi*

WAITING AT THE DOOR

Your dog shouldn't greet you at the door by knocking you over with a thud and dashing out into the street. This "trick" is not only a matter of teaching your dog good manners. His safety is also at stake.

Teach your dog not to leave the house without the release word OKAY. To do this, begin with him in the area of the door on his leash. Have someone open the door, and when he bolts forward jerk him back and tell him NO. Try this several times. Now tell him OKAY and walk him out. As soon as he is over the threshold, praise him. Bring him back in and try again. If he's too shrewd to bolt out and too dignified to slink out, have your assistant whistle to him. Don't call him by name, for then he should go. If he responds, again jerk him back and tell him NO. Once again, as you step over the threshold, tell him OK and praise him for going out. This is enough for a first session. As long as you and he are out, now you can take him for a little walk. If you don't, he's liable to think you're daft for having him go in and out so many times without going anywhere.

Continue to practice this exercise a couple of times a week by design. But also use every legitimate opportunity to work on it. Whenever you walk your dog, tell him OKAY as you go through the door, then praise him. When company comes, snap on the leash before you open the door. If he bolts, jerk him back. This exercise won't take up much of your time and is a nice safety feature. The fact that you can use it as a trick is only secondary.

Once your little darling seems to be doing well, try these sessions with his leash on but dropped. If he doesn't know you're still on the ball, he'll try to take off and cruise the neighborhood. Simply step on the leash and change his mind. When you're certain you've gotten through to him, try this without a leash on him, since that is how he's apt to be when you usually answer your bell. Have your hand firmly on the doorknob so that if he still doubts your control, you can slam the door closed—pronto. If you bump him in the nose (moderately, please!), all the better. Your job should be complete because he won't forget your hidden powers next time.

7. Useful Tricks

You do things for your dog, right? You do helpful things, loving things, cheerful things, things that could save his life. Can you think of any reason he shouldn't do the same for you? Neither can we. He can save you time and energy. He can take a little hassle out of your busy life. He can amuse and delight you—even more than he does right now. Read on and see how.

BRING YOUR DISH

This cute trick is also handy if you are tight for time. If it saves you only a half minute a day, that's over three hours a year! Think of what you could do with three hours right now!

If your precious darling is a St. Bernard who eats out of a ten-pound ceramic planter, please get him another dish for this trick. You can use a little plastic cup like the kind you get with takeout food—or a stainless steel mixing bowl that has a ring on each side. You cannot, of course, use a weighted dog dish. Experiment. Make sure before you begin that your dog can pick up the dish you ask him to bring to you.

Take the dish and, guess what? Toss it. Tell your terrific retriever TAKE IT. When your dog fetches the dish, plop a dog biscuit into it, praise her, and tell her OKAY so that she knows she can eat her reward. Try this a few more times. Your dog doesn't have to be Einstein to catch on. Begin to tell Fanny TAKE IT. BRING YOUR DISH. She's gifted, right? So why not increase her vocabulary? Now begin to ask her to bring her dish without tossing it. Have the biscuits ready. Shake the box if necessary. If she wants a treat, she'll get her dish—on the double. Drop in the biscuit and praise her.

Now Fanny can get her dish when it's chow time. We bet you won't have to practice this very often. When she hears the dog chow rattling, you probably won't have to say one word. Start planning to fill that extra three hours. We hear there's a swell movie in the neighborhood.

Now Fanny can get her dish when it's chow time.

ANSWER THE PHONE

This is not as practical as it sounds. While it is a cute trick, it can be an impressive one if handled properly. The telephone rings and Gunther rushes over to the desk, jumps up on the chair, puts his forequarters squarely in the center of the desk, and reaches down to pick up the receiver in his mouth. Once it's off the hook, Gunther drops it onto the desk and barks "Hello" into the mouthpiece. Impressive? Yes! It is merely a variation of retrieving.

Start off with your phone on the floor. Pick up the receiver and tell Gunther TAKE IT. Try this again once or twice. Now put the receiver back on the hook and tell Gunther TAKE IT. From this point on it is a simple matter to slowly move the telephone back to where it belongs—first to the desk chair, then to the edge of the desk and finally farther back on the desk. Gunther has been learning to pick up the receiver on the command TAKE IT. Now we are ready to increase his vocabulary and make the trick more impressive. Tell Gunther TAKE IT, ANSWER THE PHONE. After a little practice, just tell him ANSWER THE PHONE. Cover for him if he hesitates—TAKE IT, GUNTHER. I THINK IT'S FOR YOU!

"It's for you." *Clio Tekel—Weimaraner*

Do you want Gunther to answer the phone when it rings? Probably not. What happens when he is alone in the house and the telephone rings? As thorough as this book is, it does not teach Gunther how to take messages. Gunther will probably misspell half the names. You know dogs! Stick with this: the phone rings, you say ANSWER THE PHONE. After he picks up the receiver, tell him OUT. He will drop the receiver onto the desk and you will tell him SPEAK! Once he has the whole routine down pat, you'll start getting a lot more phone calls. Everyone will want to talk to Gunther.

BARK TO GO OUT

Everyone but everyone wants his dog to bark when he has to go out. Can he? Why not? But before we tell you the steps to follow, here are some thoughts to ponder. If your dog gets walked when he barks to request it, why can't he decide to go out at three in the morning? Why can't he decide to bark to go out when you're not home? And what does happen when he barks to go out and you just can't—you're in the bathtub, on the phone, sleeping, just plain not available? It helps your sanity to have your dog on a walking schedule, humane to him and convenient for you. Once he is, then yes, it makes sense for him to bark to go out to make minor changes in his schedule and to cover emergencies. Then, too, you can perform with him, asking BUTCH, DO YOU WANT TO GO OUT? and having him clearly verbalize his desire.

Have you taught Butch to bark on command? Follow the instructions in SPEAK, COUNT, ADD (see Chapter 11). Fine. Now sharpen his skill. Practice so that he'll speak for a biscuit or simply speak on command. Now ask him BUTCH, DO YOU WANT TO GO OUT? *SPEAK* TO GO OUT. The second he barks, snap on his leash and walk him. If he's reluctant, hold up the leash and ask him to SPEAK TO GO OUT. If he won't, don't. When he does, out for a stroll. Every time you are going to walk him on his schedule or off it, ask him to speak to go out. The magic of his voice will open the door and get you moving. He'll catch on after a short while. Low-key this one, working on it when he's due for an outing. Expect it to take a few weeks for him to get the point, but then he'll remember it forever. If he barks to go out every ten minutes, don't blame us. We warned you.

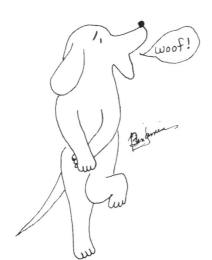

He'll bark to cover emergencies.

RING THE BELL TO COME IN

This trick is taught by hit or miss, literally. Remember we told you when you were teaching your dog to SAY YOUR PRAYERS that you would be using some of those commands again? This is one of those times. Your rever-

Practical. *Oliver Benjamin, C.D.—Golden Retriever*

ent dog learned **PAWS UP** to properly say his prayers. Now we'll do a variation on that command to teach him to let you know when he's ready to come in. But first, a word from your mother: unless your dog is spectacularly obedient, he should never be out alone. If you perimeter-train him, that is, train him to stay on your property, he may still decide not to. Pehaps he'll get his copy of the *Doggy Daily* and find out that there is a bitch in heat close by. This temptation will be likely to override your training. Or he may just spot another dog close by and want to take a romp. Dogs love to wander, explore, see the world. Don't worry, he'll send you a postcard. But we know his safety is all important to you. You don't want a postcard—you want your dog. So use this trick merely as a fine and flashy trick when you bring Snowflake home from her walk—or—Sorry! Fence your yard and turn this amazing trick into something really practical.

If your yard is fenced and your dog is safe, it can save you miserable outings in the rain late at night. On Sunday mornings, you can pad to the door, half asleep, and let Snowflake out for a romp. Instead of scratching the paint off your door or sounding off and irritating your neighbors, she will obediently ring the bell when she's ready to join you for hot rolls and the Sunday paper. Now that your dog's safety is assured, we'll gladly teach you this astounding trick.

Take Snowflake for a walk first so that she is not pulling away and distracted when you are trying to teach her something new. When you return home, clue in a cohort, your kids, wife, husband, pal, to be ready to open the door promptly and offer a treat when the bell rings. Approach your door, tap the doorbell, and command **PAWS UP**. An energetic tone will help. Encourage your dog to place her paws right on the bell, but initially

Classy.

praise her just for standing up where you tell her to. Say PAWS UP, RING THE BELL. Have your co-conspirator watching so that he doesn't open the door for your ring, only Snowflake's. PAWS UP, GOOD GIRL and you ring the bell. If Snowflake hits it once, by design or by accident, the door should open to ebullient praise and a great treat. Do not repeat the trick now.

Whenever you are in the mood to stay outside a few minutes longer than usual, repeat the trick. Once Snowflake rings the bell, in she goes to a grand reception. If you've just taught her to bark to go out, she'll catch on to this variation even faster. As she is getting more accurate, drop PAWS UP and tell her RING THE BELL. If you are alone, prepare your key and open the door quickly. Immediately praise Snowflake. Once she gets good at this, you can get her a job as a door-to-door saleslady. Now, if your yard is fenced, you can let her out and wait for the buzz.

What if your Snowflake is too short to reach the bell? You can't have everything. If you don't want to go out and buy a taller dog for this trick, place a box under the bell. Pat the box, telling her UP. Continue as above. Make sure the box is very steady or she won't want to get up on it.

With a fenced yard and a trick dog, you're in business. Watch your friends' faces when she barks to go out and then rings the bell to come in. It should be well worth the time and effort involved.

PICK THINGS UP

Are you in fact exploiting your dog if you get him to do little chores for you around the house? Did you know that most dogs were bred for work of some kind or another—and that the majority of them are among the nation's unemployed. The average dog is bored silly and never gets a chance to use his fabulous brain. By all means put your hound to work—and your working dog, terrier, toy, sporting dog, and nonsporting dog, too.

It is said that the older we get the wiser we get. But is it said that the older we get the slower we get, the less active, the heavier, the more out of breath, the more tired? Well, if it isn't said, it should be! If you're the rule, we're going to teach you how to teach Nelson to pick things up for you. And gosh, will you appreciate him late at night when you're pooped (this is before your crash diet and jogging program)? If you're overworked or overweight, this is for you. And if you're not the rule but the exception, we'll teach you how to pick up after Nelson. See, we're flexible.

At the risk of getting boring, you know darn well your dog has to retrieve for this trick. That will be true with any trick that requires him to carry something in his mouth. If you've done that well and taught him any of the other retrieving tricks, this trick will be virtually no work. Well, hardly any.

Begin with something familiar to Nelson, something he has already retrieved for you. Drop your eyeglass case and tell him NELSON, TAKE IT. If he does, experiment with other objects. Be practical. Drop things you'd drop anyway and want him to get for you. Why crawl under the table for a fork when Nelson could retrieve it?

And what if he just sits there looking at you like you're daft? Try again. This time, put some energy into it. Toss your eyeglass case and tell him TAKE IT, GOOD BOY, TAKE IT, THAT'S MY GOOD BOY. If he's doing well, try a few new things at each session. If you make it fun for him, he'll be more interested. Each toss, let the object land closer to you. Eventually drop it at your feet. Then you can try the same thing while you're sitting. Nelson should pick up your glasses, keys, silverware, pencil, etc., and bring them to you. He should hold any object he retrieves gently and let you take it without a struggle when you say OUT. Be sure to praise him warmly. He has, after all, done a big favor for you.

This small trick can be very handy. It won't show off that well in a theatrical routine, but watch your friends' faces when you or they drop something and you quietly have your dog get it for them. It will give you a deep satisfaction and sense of pride and may leave your friends sitting quietly with their mouths open. Of course, making a splash with your friends may be fun, but it isn't everything. If your cuff link rolls under the bureau or your earring lands behind the privy, your dog can save you from an awkward squeeze into an inaccessible place. You may appreciate Nelson more for this than for showing off for company. So if your trick angel is a Saint, you might want to lay in a spare Cairn Terrier or Maltese for fetching lost items from under furniture and keeping you out of trouble.

WAIT AT THE CURB

Having Rosie wait at the curb until told to go ahead will be useful for you. If you are holding her leash and juggling packages as well, you won't want her dashing ahead off the curb and into the street against the light. It will be useful to your dog because it may well save her life. Is this a trick? To the uninitiated, it will look like one. But tricks and good obedience are hard to separate. All our tricks are chock full of training secrets. And isn't the most important "trick" for any dog owner that of keeping his dog healthy, safe, and obedient? Onward and upward.

Of course, your dog should be heeling when out for a stroll. Rosie is walking calmly at your left side, at your speed, and you come to a curb. If she's heeling well, she will stop and sit automatically when *you* stop at the curb. Practice stopping at all *down* curbs for at least one week. The Seeing Eye has their dogs stop at *up* curbs as well so that the sightless owners won't trip.

Tricks and good obedience are hard to separate. *Muffin Smith—Scottish Terrier, and Powder Hillman—West Highland White Terrier*

For our trick, we want to stop Rosie from daydreaming along into traffic, so she won't need to stop when you're *leaving* the street—only before stepping off the sidewalk onto it. Once you accustom Rosie to stopping at the curb, walk ahead and this time proceed without your stop. She will no doubt plod right along, silly dog. Respond immediately. Tell her NO, SHAME! Place her back on the sidewalk and have her sit. Tap the curb with your foot and tell her SIT. Praise her, tell her to Heel and cross the street. Continue in this manner until Rosie has the idea of stopping and sitting before stepping off the sidewalk. This is a great trick if you live in a busy city, especially if you walk your dog off a leash. For added safety, if you live in the suburbs, you can have Rosie respond with a sit before she leaves your driveway.

Practice whenever you are out walking. This will take no more time than your normal daily strolls. And remember, if she is a curbed city dog, she still must sit first before going into the street to attend to her needs. It'll be safer and saner since *you* can check first for buses or cars about to pull in near the curb.

OPEN AND CLOSE THE DOOR

Don't you wish that when your dog poked open the bedroom or bathroom door, he'd have the ability and courtesy to close it, too? You'll need a few things in order to teach this trick well. First, you'll need a dog that can reach a doorknob. Second, unless you have the patience of Job, you'll need some French doors—or at least some French doorknobs. By using the command PAWS UP, you can teach Houdini to hook a paw over this type of latch, take a step backward, and open the door. If the door you begin with is the door he exits from, so much the better. Work for a few minutes before his walk and then let him reap his reward—a long stroll. He will be in an excited frame of mind and will do almost anything to get outside. Don't *practice* —just *use* the command. PAWS UP, OPEN THE DOOR, GOOOOOD BOY. Houdini's no dope; he'll catch on. In fact, he may catch on better than you imagine—so keep the doors locked or you'll find Houdini taking French leave through your French doors at will.

If you have standard round doorknobs and cannot replace even one with French doorknobs, you'll have a tougher job. If we know you, you won't mind! Wrap and secure a piece of foam rubber around the knob. The dog will scratch up the knob with his teeth if it isn't covered. It will also be easier for him if the knob is made less slippery. Now tape the snap of the door open with adhesive tape so that the door will open more easily. At first, Houdini will just grasp the knob and pull. Later, he can learn to twist it first. For round knobs, your Houdini must be a retriever. You will tell him TAKE IT, OPEN THE DOOR. Keep him excited. Keep talking to him. In his excitement, he will pull on the knob. If the snap is taped, he will succeed easily and you can praise him and walk him. As he learns what to do and enjoys helping to speed his outings, you can remove the tape from the snap. Once motivated, he will pull and twist in his desire to OPEN THE DOOR and go for a delicious walk.

CLOSE THE DOOR is a useful trick as well as an interesting one. It can be taught as a variation of PAWS UP and with or without teaching the dog to open a door. Approach a partially opened door with Houdini and tell him PAWS UP, CLOSE THE DOOR. Soon you will be able to drop the PAWS UP command, but initially it tells the dog what to do. Praise Houdini warmly when he shuts the door for you. As you can see, new tricks are often "made" by changing the command. It's a lot easier than teaching a new trick and it looks just as good. By observing your dog's behavior and thinking about the various possibilities of each command, you will find that there are dozens of other tricks you can invent and teach in record time.

Now that Houdini can do an escape act at one door, work with him at all the doors in your house. In this way, you can have many practical rewards for your work and his. Next time there's a draft when you're in the tub, you can just call upon Houdini. With luck, he'll close the bathroom door. If he's silly, he may open the front door instead and let the neighbors in. So, as with other tricks, make sure he works his magic on command only.

TV ON, TV OFF

More than likely, if your dog, Marconi, watches a little TV while you are out, burglars will assume that you are home and pass you by. Of course, merely leaving the set on all evening won't fool a clever crook. But an electric timer can do this service for you as well or better than a dog. Our fantasy is to collapse into a comfortable chair and let Marconi do all the work. Getting up to change the channel or shut off the set can be rough after a hard day at the loop end of the leash!

In keeping with our philosophy, the most results for the least effort, use a TV that has a simple button that turns the set on or off with the same motion. Or if you really want it easy, get a floor button—the step-on kind used on lamps—and hook that up to your TV. Getting the dog to hit the floor button with his paw when you say TV is no big trick. But even if you never astonish your neighbors with Marconi's skill, you'll love it yourself—especially when your dog shuts off your set at commercial time.

When working with an on/off button on the TV set itself, make sure the set is on a heavy table and not a stand on wheels. Tell Marconi PAWS UP! TURN IT. Since he will hit the button to turn it on or off, you need only add ON or OFF when showing off. With either kind of switch, Marconi will have to make the connection between hitting the button and hearing the TV cut on or off. This will take him some time, so be sure to praise well for each try. Repeat the command TURN IT as he stands up near the TV. Encourage him to hit the switch. When he does, let your praise flow and end the session. Work for very short periods of time, preferably when you are watching TV anyway and the commercial break comes! That way you and Marconi won't be missing anything.

This isn't the easiest trick in the world to teach your dog. Marconi will be winging it at first. It will take some time for the sound change on the TV to let him know he has been successful. Prior to that, he'll just be pawing at the TV because you are asking him to. In fact, make sure that he does do it only when you ask him to. Otherwise, he might keep turning the TV on and off every time he wants to hear what a great dog he is. If you're a real worker and get him to change the channel and fetch you a cool beer, please send all details for our sequel, *Son of Dog Tricks*.

8. Jumping Tricks

There are numerous, flashy tricks your dog can perform if he learns to jump on command. You must proceed slowly and build his confidence. It is most important for the dog to feel he can take that jump safely and land on something familiar that will support him. And it is equally important that he never finds out that there's an alternative to the jump. Whether he's to sail off a ladder into your waiting arms or jump through a hoop or over a stick, he must feel that jumping is the *only* way to travel. And, remembering that cowards die a thousand deaths, etc., you'll spend sufficient time making him believe that he's the closest thing possible to an eagle, despite the fact that he's not even a bird dog!

JUMPING—BASIC TRAINING

The easiest way to start your dog jumping is by placing a board in a doorway. Here the situation is set up so that if the dog wants to get from one room to another, he will have to go over the board. He cannot go around it or under it. He cannot find another entrance into the room. And what will make him want to go into that room in the first place—you will, you clever devil!

Begin by taking the jump with your dog. Take a long running start, and as you approach the board lift slightly up and forward with the leash and tell him PUNCH, OVER. Jump with him and fall upon him with kisses and exuberant praise. Most dogs love jumping and it is indeed great exercise for any healthy dog—as long as the jump is not too high. If your dog is not dysplastic, arthritic, or pregnant and if he has no back problems or problems with his legs, he should be able to jump at least one and one half times his height at the shoulder. This means that the average large dog can jump around three feet or better. If your sweetie won't jump the board with you, perhaps you're starting with too high a jump. Since we want to build

Punch's confidence, let's try again, with encouragement and with a lower board if necessary. Don't worry. Once he gets the hang of it, he'll be sailing over just about anything. And so again, a word from your mother. Great as these tricks are, if you are in hock up to your nose for that chain link fence that surrounds your yard and your dog, think twice. A fence is often a psychological barrier to a dog as well as a physical deterrent. He may be able to jump four feet and still stay behind a three-foot fence—as long as there's nothing *too* interesting on the other side. But let a female in heat wiggle down your road or perhaps just a chasable-looking tomcat, and your "bird" may just fly the coop. After all, you are going to teach him how. Should you? Probably yes, but contemplate the above first.

Now, here we are, you and Punch and us, back in the doorway with the board. Put old Punch on a Sit Stay in one room, facing the board, step over the board into the next room, holding his leash, and, taking a big breath, tell him PUNCH, COME, OVER, GOOD BOY. Yes? THAT'S MY GOOD BOY. And continue. Now you can stand with Punch near the board and send *him* to the next room, clever little tyke, he's catching on. Tell him OVER . . . OVER. He should jump away and then back toward you. And, of course, you'll tell him he's terrific.

Now we can get fancy.

JUMP THROUGH A HOOP

Place your hoop in the doorway. Why make it easy for Punch to make a mistake? He knows how to jump and what the word OVER means, but he

"Hup!" *Dawn Mitchell—Poodle*

may not like going *under* the top of the hoop. With you in one room and Punch in the other, draw his leash through the hoop, which is sitting on the ground in the doorway. Call Punch and have him come to you through the hoop. If he seems spooked by it, talk him through: ATTA BOY, THAT'S MY GOOD BOY. COME, COME ON, BABY, etc. Pet him. Praise him. Try it again. Once Punch is walking through the hoop as if it is not even there, raise it a bit, still keeping it in the doorway. When Punch will easily and willingly go both ways with the hoop one foot off the ground, you may leave the doorway and work with the hoop held in your hand.

The principle is as follows: the dog may not avoid the hoop to get to you or elsewhere. It is your job, not his, to make sure this is what happens. Ask Punch to jump through the hoop. If he begins a journey around it, tell him NO, OVER as you move the hoop so that it is still in front of him. If you have it two feet high and he begins to bend his hairy little head to go under it—NO, OVER and lower the hoop. Sneaky? Well, it's easier than raising the dog!

Continue to build his confidence with the hoop. Each practice session, give him a warm-up with the hoop quite low before you ask him to jump as high as he is able. And work at this when you're in an "up" mood so that you can share your energy with Punch and give him lots of praise and encouragement.

JUMP OVER A PERSON OR ANOTHER DOG

This is one of the goofiest of jumping stunts, but it comes early in the section because it is as easy to teach as it is funny to watch. Ask a friend to help you and warm up Punch with some hoop jumping for a few minutes. Now stretch out on the floor and get comfortable. Have your friend take a running start and jump over you with Punch, making sure to tell him PUNCH, OVER. Please, don't have a klutzy friend help you with this one!

Once Punch will jump over your body with your friend, proceed with the steps above—sending him over both ways on his own. Practice and praise.

Now you can get even goofier. Lie down and tell Punch OVER. As he jumps, roll back toward where he was coming from, calling to him GOOD BOY, OVER. Repeat until tired. You can line up a few friends on the floor —surely your dog can jump the width of more than one person. Or put your other dog, Judy, on a Down Stay and have Punch jump over Judy. If you do have two dogs and you really want to have your talent shine, this can expand into a real circus routine.

Teach both dogs to jump over each other, slowly and patiently as above. Now change the routine as follows: Punch jumps over Judy and then lies down. Judy gets up and jumps over Punch, who rolls over toward where she was coming from as you did (*see* ROLL OVER, in Chapter 4). Judy lies down immediately after her jump. Punch now jumps and they keep reversing. If this is done correctly, they will remain in virtually the same area and you will look like Clyde Beatty. Do it!

JUMP OVER MY ARM

Having a dog jump over your resting body, your arm, your extended leg, or your head looks a heck of a lot flashier and harder to do than it is. In short, it's our kind of trick.

After a short warm-up, have a friend take your dog, on leash, and approach you as you kneel with one arm extended. Tell the dog PUNCH, OVER and have your friend assist, if necessary, by pulling the leash slightly up and forward. Always make sure you release the pressure on the leash as soon as the dog is doing his jump so that you don't end up correcting him accidentally for proper obedience. Continue as above, practicing to make your dog feel comfortable with this new routine. If he is large enough, or you are very short, have him graduate to jumping over your arm as you stand. Or, for variety, link hands with a friend to form a "fence" and let him jump that.

VARIATIONS WITH PEOPLE PROPS

By now Punch should know what you want when he hears the command OVER and sees an obstacle in this way. So now you can play further with obstacles, as long as you watch your dog's reactions. If he's scared or spooked, go back to jumping things he likes and build him up again. Always give him a warm-up. Be generous with your praise. And keep sessions short so as not to tire him or make him sore. It's even a good idea, whenever starting a new routine, to let him investigate the "landing area" before he takes off.

If you've got great legs, put on a pair of dark stockings and, holding one of your gorgeous gams out, tell Punch OVER. (And guys, leave this one to the ladies. If *you've* got great legs, take up tennis.)

Bending down on your knees, make a circle of your arms and hold them so that your dog can jump through the circle as he would a hoop. Now raise one leg and place your foot flat on the floor. Let Punch return and jump over your bent leg. Now crouch and let him jump over your back. Get it? If you have a loony little Terrier or a Poodle with energy to burn and a silly personality, you have it made. All the better if you are agile, too. At every jump, change position and present a new obstacle. This set of jumping tricks will have the look of circus—fast work, comedy, and a lot of activity. Your one dog may look like twenty if he works fast. If he's really a little clown, he can change hats between jumps!

STICK JUMPING

Stick jumping is a variation on the above work, this time with a prop. You can use any straight stick, a cane, or a painted dowel, cut to a handy

"Real show biz, kid."

length (let's say 32 inches or 81 centimeters). Hold the stick out as you would your arm and have Punch take the jump. If you've done the tricks above, no problem at all.

Now hold the stick in both hands, over your head. Do it—we're not kidding. You'll probably need help to begin this one, too. With the stick just over your head, not way up high, bend down and lean on one knee. Now have Punch learn this jump. When you and he are ready for a solo, begin with Punch on a Sit Stay across the room from you. Stand tall and hold the stick as high over your head as you can reach. As you call to him PUNCH, OVER, bend to one knee and lower your arms so that the stick is right over your head. The trick, done well, *gives the impression* that the dog is jumping high over your head while you are standing up. That's real show biz, kid. So to add to the illusion, stand up again immediately *after* he goes over you. If you do it too soon, take two aspirin, get plenty of rest, and call us in the morning.

JUMP INTO MY ARMS

This little beauty is a nice addition to the jumping package but won't work if you have a Mastiff, Newfoundland, St. Bernard, Great Pyrenees, Bernese Mountain Dog, Golden Retriever, Irish Setter, Irish Wolfhound, Scottish Deerhound, Bloodhound, Otterhound, or other large dog. (Bet you think we get paid by the word.) In other words, you need a tiny dog—unless you're King Kong. Many small dogs, when excited, will jump up and down. Get your little munchkin in a happy mood, clap over his head, hold up tidbits of food, whistle and hoot, and get him up in the air. And then—catch him. And really make a fuss. Now try again. He won't be jumping way high at first, so bend down to make your catch. Part of his reward will be getting caught and lifted up—the little ham—so he will begin to jump even higher. Continue this as a game for a few minutes every day. Now try to encourage him to begin to help—call him to come and hold out your arms. Pat your legs, hold up some food, and catch him when he jumps—whether he's doing it to get up to you or just out of excitement. As he learns that you will catch him and praise him, he's more apt to try. He may prefer it when you're seated or kneeling, so experiment. And if you love this trick and have an American Foxhound, a Saluki, a Borzoi, a Labrador Retriever, an Akita, a German Shepherd, an Old English Sheepdog, or a Boxer, buy him a little friend.

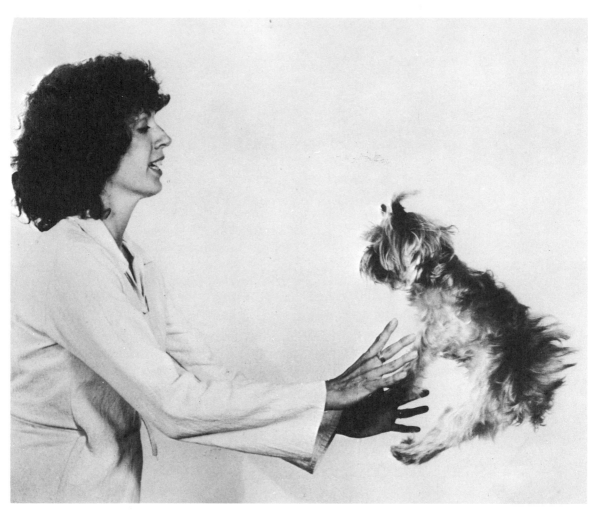

"It's a bird. It's a plane. It's Freddie!" *Freddie Gold—Yorkshire Terrier*

9. Agility Tricks

These tricks are not for the casual, living-room dog trainer. If you love to show off for your friends and get a few laughs with your dog, you can have a party with many of our other flashy but easy tricks. The tricks in this special section have several things in common—most of them are difficult, all of them require special equipment or props, you'll need above average skill as a handler, and your dog should be especially well trained and as well seasoned as possible. It would be unfair to take a "green" dog and ask him to climb a ladder or scale a wall. Your student should be confident, well behaved, and in excellent physical condition before you attempt these feats of agility. However, if he is and if you do, have no doubt that you and your dog will become an impressive pair. These tricks are unusually breathtaking and will definitely put you and your dog onto an undeniably higher level of achievement. So if you are both solid workers and in need of some excitement, please do read on.

NOTE: Special care should be taken to make sure that all the equipment used is appropriate and sound. Training should proceed slowly and methodically. Care should be taken to give the dog proper praise and sufficient relief from this difficult work.

THE TEETER-TOTTER

It isn't necessary to construct a teeter-totter or seesaw in your back yard in order to teach your dog this trick. If you live near a children's playground, you can make use of public property. After the little children are tucked in for the night, go to the playground and take your "baby" on the seesaw. Your dog will be on your left, on leash, as you approach the seesaw. Put your left foot on the down side of the seesaw and encourage your dog to climb up onto it. Most dogs will try to jump off one side or the other at first.

Take your baby on the seesaw.

Keep the leash out of his way as he works. *Harlow Maney—Bloodhound*

Tighten up on the leash so that Cheech can't jump off the teeter-totter while you are working with him. As he gets to the center of the board, bend over, scoop him up, and praise him. If Cheech is a one hundred eighty-five pound St. Bernard, do not scoop him up, but praise him right there on the seesaw. Try this two or three times in an up mood. That's enough for today. You don't have to stop dog training for the day—just knock off this exercise so that your dog doesn't get bored.

The next day, go back to the park and begin in the same way. Be sure to keep your left foot on the teeter-totter so that your dog won't run up the board and become frightened when his weight causes it to shift sides. Now when Cheech gets to the center of the board, say STEAAADY in a drawn-out, reassuring manner. With the leash in your left hand, the collar tight on Cheech's neck, reach forward and grasp the higher end of the board with your right hand. Repeat your reassuring STEAAADY as you slowly move Cheech forward and lower the raised portion of the board to the level position. Be careful to control the board so that the other side does not slam to the ground. Work carefully and slowly, continuing to talk to Cheech in a reassuring voice. Guide the board now so that it lands on the ground gently. Cheech, still under your control so that he can't jump off to the side, will continue forward down the seesaw and off. Lavish him with praise.

Once Cheech learns to do this trick with confidence, he will be able to do it rapidly. He'll be anxious to get it over with anyway and get on to the good stuff—the fuss you will make over him. But he must understand that it is necessary to pause in the middle and wait until his weight has caused the board to shift before he comes galloping down the other side. Until he learns to use enough control himself, you must keep tight control of this exercise. Once the trick is mastered, you can add your own flair to it. Outfit him in a clown suit, let him carry something in his mouth, try two small dogs—nose to tail. Then you can bring your own crowd with you to the playground or merely go during daylight hours and give the little children a thrill with your trick dog.

SCALE A WALL

The practicality of this trick is overshadowed by its impressiveness. This is an exercise used by the police and the military. In the pursuit of an evil-doer, a dog must be able to navigate any obstacle that the "varmint" might escape over, under, or through. A wall is one such obstacle. There is a difference between scaling a wall and jumping over it. When there is a low wall in the dog's way, he may jump over it. A successful jump is one in which the dog does not touch the wall as he soars over it. But what if the wall is too high? In scaling, direct contact with the wall is necessary. The wall may be impossible for the dog to clear and he will have to scramble up to go over the top. Different muscles and bones are used for this exercise and it is taught in a different way.

There is an added advantage to teaching a dog to scale. It will build his confidence and make him feel that he is a canine that can overcome obstacles. This will be a great help to you and to your dog if he is rather shy.

There are disadvantages to this exercise, too. In order to teach this trick, you will have to build a special wall and sometimes, even, have a place to store it. If you use the permanent kind of scaling wall and have it built in your back yard, at least you will have an excellent conversation piece. The second disadvantage is that this will be very hard work for your dog—particularly when he comes crashing down on the reverse side of the scaling wall. Slow-motion films of this exercise show that the dog receives a tremendous jolt when he lands. However, dogs that have been doing this arduous work for years were studied carefully and it was found that there were no serious ill effects as a direct result of the scaling. Their bodies were toughened up and conditioned to be able to take the physical stress of the work. Since your dog is not a police or military dog, we will make things easier on him. You will construct your wall for Kojak with a platform at half the maximum height on the reverse side of the scaling wall.

This trick will be physically hard on both you and Kojak. But take heart. It is not quite as difficult to teach as it will appear to anyone you show it to.

There are two types of scaling walls. One is permanent and it is cemented into the ground. It has an adjustable height, will last indefinitely, and it is easy to construct, use, and maintain. The other type does not have an adjustable height, is portable, and, when viewed from the side, it has an A-frame type appearance. Instead of adjusting the height, adjust the angle of the wall. The portable wall may seem more appealing because it would appear that you could take it with you to county fairs and demonstrations. However, it is heavy, unwieldy, it takes a beating when transported, and it should only be used on dirt surfaces. Furthermore, you'd need a rather large truck to transport it and, even then, you might not have room to squeeze in your dog! We find the permanent scaling wall with an adjustable height the best bet if you can swing it.

To start this training, begin with a height of about five feet (152 cm) if your dog is German Shepherd or Doberman sized. At this height, you will not need the platform on the reverse side. You will begin to the right of your dog so that he is in the Heel position. With leash and choke collar on, begin your dog about six feet away from the wall and talk to him in a peppy, encouraging tone. After all, he is not going to scale a wall in his sleep. Trot in place. Talk excitedly to Kojak. LET'S GET READY, KOJAK. WE'RE GOING TO DO IT. I KNOW YOU CAN DO IT, KOJAK. He won't know what on earth you expect, but he will get excited. Tell him LET'S GO and move out rapidly toward the scaling wall. As you approach it, exert an upward pressure on the leash and tell Kojak HUP! As you give the command, leash in your left hand, pull Kojak over the wall. As he comes down the

"Up, up, and . . ."

"Over the top!" *Zee Bones—German Shepherd*

other side, lavish him with praise. *But make sure at this point that the leash does not become entangled with the scaling wall.* Kojak should get praised immediately after completing the exercise. If the leash is not completely released, he would receive a jerk immediately after completing the exercise —an improper correction which would confuse him. So watch the leash and praise him energetically—WHAT A WONDERFUL BOY! THAT'S MY GOOD DOG. I KNEW YOU COULD DO IT!

Now try another time from the same direction. Don't ever let Kojak decide to go around the obstacle rather than over it. If he tries, pull him back and tell him NO. As the wall gets higher, you will need more strength, but then again, Kojak will try to goof off less. Try the wall five times the first day, but be sure that Kojak scales properly on the fifth try. Do not finish up on an improperly executed exercise. If you need an extra try to get it right, do it. If he is repeatedly getting it wrong, the fault may lie with you. It is your job to make Kojak go over the scaling wall. If you can't, rush into the house and take some vitamins and join the local Y. Your dog will not do this exercise out of love. He must know that you are able to make him scale the wall.

Each time you work, increase the number of tries by one or two. When you have Kojak successfully scaling the five-foot wall twelve times, add a plank to the obstacle. You can increase the height by four inches first, and then two inches each time afterward. After each increase, reduce the number of tries to seven and then build him back up to twelve. By now Kojak has the idea and you can progress rapidly. It is a good idea to mark the boards so that you can easily figure out the height. If you dislike math, turn to SPEAK, COUNT, ADD (see Chapter 11) and have Kojak do the addition for you. It will add some extra pizazz to the trick.

Once you have worked Kojak up to a height of five feet eight inches (173 cm), you and he will have a respectable trick. If you continue all the way to six feet (about 180 cm), you will have both a respectable and a very impressive trick. Most police dog trials require the dogs to scale a six-foot wall —so Kojak will be in good company.

If you plan to make the sky your limit, you will have to add "cheaters" to your wall. These are furring strips that will give the dog some added traction for the added height. If you are going to teach Kojak to scale a wall over six feet high, he will need the cheaters. In the case of the A-frame wall, instead of increasing the height, the angle is increased until the scaling wall is almost perpendicular to the ground. Obviously, it is impossible to get these obstacles to a ninety-degree angle.

Since people tend to exaggerate the height their dogs can scale almost as often as they will exaggerate the height and weight of their dogs, you should be aware of the record. The record height is twelve feet four inches and was set by Falko, a German Shepherd Dog, belonging to Mrs. G. Smith of Swampscott, Massachusetts. If your Kojak can break that record, let us know for our next printing.

WALK A CATWALK

The higher and narrower the catwalk, the more impressive this trick becomes. However, when you are enjoying showing off your dog with the aid of this trick, no one will be aware of the width of the catwalk. A two-foot-wide catwalk looks, to spectators, about the same as a six-inch-wide catwalk. Yet the difficulty in teaching your dog to walk the narrower path would be increased more than fourfold. So when constructing your catwalk, make it wide. It must be steady and solid. It would be very difficult to train your dog to walk a rickety catwalk, even if it were quite close to the ground. Since low, temporary catwalks would have to be quite solid in order for your dog to comfortably navigate them, when all is said and done, you will be better off constructing a high permanent one. The training might be a little more difficult at first, but it will save you the time and money involved in building several at graduated heights. Before you begin, analyze just what you plan to do with this trick. If you want to show off in your own back yard, make a solid obstacle. If you want the trick so that you can travel around and entertain local civic groups or take your trick genius to entertain the troops, you'll need something more portable. Homemade catwalks out of wood are usually not solid enough and don't stand up well. A better bet would be a professionally made aluminum catwalk that can be taken apart for travel.

If the catwalk is to be part of an obstacle course, thought should be given to the order in which these permanent obstacles are constructed. Obstacles should be placed in a sequence in which they can be well navigated. Of course, save the best for last to add a memorable flourish to your act.

With these objectives in mind, you will have a catwalk for your dog to practice on that is shoulder height or higher. Now, how will he get up to the catwalk? You can have steps leading up to the top that are sloped gradually and are closed in at the bottom. The more open the steps, the more they will frighten your dog. You may have noticed that dogs are wary of steps when they can see the ground between them. There's no need to make the approach to the catwalk more difficult than the catwalk itself. Another good solution would be a ramp. You can add some strips to the ramp to give your dog support and traction for his climb. The other end can have a ramp as well. Or you can build a platform halfway down so that he can get to the ground with two moderate jumps—a nice finish for a flashy trick.

With Fuzzy in the Heel position, slowly encourage her up the steps or ramp to the top of the catwalk. Fuzzy will be working as usual on your left side and you will be guiding her carefully with her leash and talking to her in a reassuring manner. If she seems nervous, you can stop and pet her and tell her that everything is okay. But do not let her jump off the catwalk! Stop her, slow her down, reassure her. You can even give her a treat if you think

it will help to calm her. Take your time. Rushing through any of these agility tricks will accomplish nothing. Slowly, slowly work her to the end of the
catwalk. Carefully let her jump to the platform and then down to the ground.
Now you can praise her profusely. She has just done the most remarkable
thing any dog could do. If she enjoys the petting and the fuss you are making
over her and if she doesn't seem overly nervous, you can take one or two
more shots at the catwalk in this first session. If the trip has upset her, let her
knock off for the day. Slow repetitions with a lot of praise will have Fuzzy,
in a short period of time, rushing up the catwalk to do her thing.

Even for human beings, overcoming obstacles does wonders for the ego.
And so it is with dogs, too. Taking your dog through an obstacle course will
build her confidence in herself and in you. It may help a shy dog to blossom
forth. It may even help a shy owner to feel more confident as a dog trainer
and a performer. Though the work is difficult at first and the construction
may be time-consuming and somewhat costly, these tricks may offer some
special fringe benefits to both master and dog.

CLIMB A LADDER

Here is a trick that is as hard as it looks. It is not made any easier by putting the ladder at a lower angle because your dog will still be frightened
when he sees the ground between the rungs. Pick your ladder carefully—a
painter's ladder is a good bet or an aluminum extendable ladder will do.
Using the same ladder and the same location will make the mastering of this
skill easier for your dog. At first, Sherpa will be twisting and shaking when
he climbs, so make sure the ladder is very steady.

With Sherpa in the Heel position, collar and leash on, approach the ladder, pat the first step, and say CLIMB. With any degree of training under
his belt, Sherpa will respond by putting his paw on the first rung. The easy
part of this trick is now over. The second rung may present a bit of a problem. Command CLIMB as you gently pull up on the choke collar and lift
his legs onto the second rung. So far, so good. But the real difficulty comes
when Sherpa has to place his hindquarters on the ladder. Because of the
confirmation of his skull, he cannot see the steps when he looks down as you
and I could. This will make him less steady until his confidence is built.
Keep forcing the collar upward, saying CLIMB! Don't expect miracles the
first day. When Sherpa is halfway up the ladder, pick him up and lavish him
with praise. He was scared, but he did it for you, that terrific dog.

It is most important that Sherpa does not fall off the ladder. A bad experience would give him a real setback. He may even try to jump off, but don't
let him! He'd invariably hurt himself by not clearing the ladder, or it might
even fall over as he jumped. Once he is climbing to the top and under good
control, you may want to teach him to jump off the platform of the painter's

ladder—on your command. You won't want him scurrying up to the top and jumping on his own. It will take you time to get around to that side of the ladder and get ready to catch him. If you are using an extension ladder, you can have it go right to a low window. Then Sherpa won't have to jump at all—he can go right up the ladder and into your house. Of course, when you're not working with him, you'll be sure to remove the ladder. Otherwise someone less welcome might climb the ladder and go right into your house!

As Sherpa progresses in his training and you progress in your ability to handle this difficult exercise, you will reach a point where you can toss the leash over the top of the ladder and pull downward to aid Sherpa in his climb. Keep the leash taut but not tight. A loose leash might become entangled in Sherpa's legs, causing a dangerous situation. If the leash is too tight, Sherpa won't have time to secure his footing. Be careful—you are hauling precious cargo.

The first time you try this trick, do it only once. Do not work up to more than two or three repetitions until Sherpa has it down pat. Don't work to the point where you put too much stress on your dog. This exercise is very pressured for him and you will not want to make him shy away from the ladder. Done properly and slowly, he will learn to enjoy this because it pleases you so much. So be sure to offer exuberant praise every time the task is accomplished. After all, your dog is doing a very brave thing at your request.

JUMP INTO THE CAR

Why on earth would you want your dog to jump into your car? If you're a professional trainer and having Oliver show his stuff, it's a dramatic finale for your act. If you're a professional ham and showing off with your dog, it's also a dramatic finale for your act. If you teach only this trick and have no act, you'll get ooh's and ah's on the street when you return with Oliver from the post office and, making sure your car window is open all the way, command JUMP INTO THE CAR. Passers-by will see him sail in through the window and think he knows every trick in the book. Is there a practical side to this trick? You know us—whenever possible, the answer is YES! Suppose your car is a hatchback or station wagon. If your Oliver weighs seventy-five pounds, you won't want to lift him into the back. If it's wet out and he has to enter the car through the door and jump on and over all the seats to get to his spot, you and your passengers will be sitting on mud. So JUMP INTO

When he lands, take him for a ride. *Oliver Benjamin, C.D.—Golden Retriever*

THE CAR may be a perfect solution for you. For very little work, it's guaranteed to make you look like an ace dog trainer, too.

We're not trying to confuse you, but it's easier on your dog if you teach him to jump *out* of your car before he learns to jump into it. Also, before you begin, make sure you distinguish your normal GET IN THE CAR from this JUMP INTO THE CAR so that he doesn't take a flying leap into a closed window next time you're in a rush. This is no place to mumble. Clearly emphasize the GET or the JUMP.

Begin with Oliver on his leash. You have already obedience-trained him and taught him several tricks so he's an apt student and an ardent listener. Tell him to GET IN THE CAR. Open the window *all the way* and draw his leash through it. Now, encouragingly and with energy, call him to you. You can give a slight assist with the leash, but don't drag him out. He may peer over the edge to check out the landing area, but he should jump out quite easily. Try this a few times—with big praise—and then begin the reverse. With the car window still open all the way, tap the car near the window and tell him JUMP INTO THE CAR. Again, he's likely to want to stand up and check out the other side. Let him. He may even make a few false starts. If he's really unsure of himself, teaching him to JUMP THROUGH A HOOP first will be a big help. Now—give him a running start. As you near the car, tell him JUMP INTO THE CAR and boost him a little with the leash. Follow with enthusiastic praise and a ride.

If you own a station wagon or hatchback, put one of your darling children in the back with a few dog biscuits. Open the back as far as it goes and tell him JUMP INTO THE CAR, FIND VICKI. Vicki can start calling Oliver to come to her and she can show him the biscuit. Unless he's a tiny toy or a long, long low-slung model, he'll oblige. Practice when taking him for a ride. That way, he'll get a double reward for his agility. And what if he's too small? We already told you to get a taller dog to Ring the Bell to Come In. If you didn't get one then, and you won't get one now, try another trick.

10. Circus Tricks

What makes those little circus dogs so energetic and appealing? What keeps them going two shows a day, seven days a week? Part of the secret is applause. Like people, dogs work for applause. Many dogs love nothing better than to ham it up before an audience, the larger the better. Some dogs will make pleasant or amusing additions to their routines in response to audience feedback. Perhaps you've even noticed your own dog repeating a goof that once got him a laugh. If your dog is capable of cracking jokes, by all means teach him some circus tricks and let him ad-lib.

Circus dogs, not unlike yours and ours, need to be seasoned troupers. Your dog will need gradual exposure to crowds before he thrives on being a crowd pleaser. As you build his repertoire of tricks, take him out for strolls in your local shopping center. Work him through the local hardware store or five-and-dime. Take him with you to a flea market (no pun intended) or sidewalk sale. In this way, you can help prepare him for life under the spotlights. Even if your little clown never decides to run away with the circus, it will help season him for performing in front of Aunt Mimi and Uncle Dick or at a special dinner for the Green Bay Packers. Whatever audience you choose, if you play your cards right, your dog will not only perform like a trouper, but he'll enjoy every minute of it and ask to come back. So have a good time—as he will—and don't forget to clap and cheer.

JUMP THROUGH A PANEL

This is a variation of jumping through a hoop or of stick jumping. It adds a dramatic touch to any demonstration, particularly if the paper panel has a picture on it. But this dramatic trick has one enormous disadvantage. Each time your dog jumps through the panel, it has to be replaced. Usually, the panel is put on a hoop. Rather than making one, you can purchase a Hula-

Hoop. And while you're shopping, stock up on a ton of this tissue paper in various colors.

Do not begin by pasting the tissue paper on the Hula-Hoop. Your first job is to get your dog to go through the hoop. (See Jumping Tricks, Chapter 8) When this trick is mastered, you can begin to close in the circle of the hoop with *strands* of tissue paper rather than a solid panel. Attach the strands only to the top of the hoop, using rubber cement. If little Jim takes this change in his stride, begin to paste the strands to the bottom of the hoop as well. Gradually add strands to the hoop as you give Jim his workouts each day. If you have a nice feel for design, make a rainbow effect by using strands of variegated colors. Now you have an impressive trick even before your dog is jumping through a solid panel of tissue paper. By all means practice in front of an audience at this stage of the work.

Jim is almost ready for the big time—or the big top. By now you have so many strands on the hoop that it is nearly covered. Try him next on a solid barrier of tissue, but rip a hole in the center so that he can see where he's going and thus feel more confident. As you can no doubt see, the hardest part of this trick is keeping a supply of tissue paper on hand and replacing the panels. Once Jim will jump through the panel with the rip in the middle, he is ready to try a solid panel. But the trick itself will be sufficiently flashy at any of several stages. Once you and he have made it through to the solid panel, you can really make an impressive impression.

If Jim takes to panel jumping like a duck to water, you may want to take the trick a step further. You can rig up several hoops in a row and have Jim take a flying leap through all of them. Or you can add a colorful costume to the routine. He can even jump through the panel carrying something in his mouth. Plain or fancy, this trick is sure to win cheers for you and your jumping Jim.

ROLL A BARREL

The Sing Along record you didn't know what to do with can now come off the shelf. Put on "The Beer Barrel Polka" and you can have a barrel of fun with your friends and your trick dog. This trick will make your dog's repertoire begin to look like a polished act. The use of color, music, and equipment will make any act have that professional touch. And this beauty has the music, the gaily decorated prop, and all the pizazz you could ask for.

But, there is a disadvantage to equipment in any act. It is expensive and difficult to transport. In addition, it is getting tougher and tougher to get a barrel today. The traditional wooden barrels that took a cooper artisan to construct and repair are being replaced by cardboard and plastic. These have the advantage that they are more likely to roll straight, but if you plan to do twenty-six weeks on the road, a cardboard barrel will not hold up. Choose the size of the barrel to suit the proportions of your dog. An overly large barrel will obscure a tiny dog. For a small fry, the barrels used for swimming-pool chlorine supplies can be ideal. The right size is important, but don't worry about decorating the barrel until you have your act together.

Begin your work on a level surface. A paved area is better than grass, which will have some uneven spots. Begin on your dog's left. During most of the training you have done with your dog, he has been on *your* left. Here it is reversed for the sake of flexibility. When performing, your dog should remain between you and your audience. The dog will roll the barrel across the stage, rather than toward the audience or away from it. You will want to be able to change sides easily to stay upstage from your dog without confusing him. Since he is used to working at your left, it is preferable to get him used to working at your right during the initial phases of this new trick. Bacchus is on leash and wearing a choke collar. The excess leash is neatly folded up in your hand to keep it out of the way. In your left hand you will hold a stick. Your left foot will stretch forward to keep the barrel from rolling forward. Now tell Bacchus to put his PAWS UP. Tap the barrel with your stick as you give the command. As you do this, pull up and forward with the leash and encourage him to get his feet up on the barrel. Once he does, loosen the leash and praise him. Speak calmly to him to reassure him as you work. You do not want him to get fearful of the barrel.

The barrel is still, held in place by your foot, and now Bacchus has all four feet up on the barrel. Command ROLL, hold up the leash for control, and tap one of his forequarters with the stick. Bacchus will lift that leg and you can release the pressure on his collar. Now, like Peg Leg Bates, skip along forward on one foot. Tap your dog's other leg as you gently pull up on the leash. As he places the first leg down and lifts the other off the barrel,

PAWS UP.

Encourage him to get his feet up on the barrel. *Snoopy Simoni—Mixed Breed*

release pressure with the leash. Now pause and praise. Work slowly. As he alternates lifting his feet, allow the barrel to roll forward. Each time you tap him gently on the leg, repeat the command ROLL. Each time he positions his foot back on the barrel, tell him what a good dog he is. Once he has the idea, you can pick up the tempo.

If Bacchus is the ham we hope he is, you will soon be able to work without a collar and leash. Then you can rely upon the stick alone to cue your dog. Once he hops up on the barrel with enthusiasm and begins to get it rolling, you can dispense with the stick. By then, Bacchus will just have to see his barrel and he'll be ready to roll it out and give you a barrel of fun. Now's the time to think of a colorful decorating scheme that will look its best when the barrel is on the move. Be sure, if your dog is to dress to the teeth for his performance, that his outfit is co-ordinated with your barrel decorations. Now you and Bacchus are ready for an agent and worldwide bookings.

DRAG A BOX

In this interesting variation of Tug It (Chapter 17) your dog will learn to drag a box by pulling on a rope. Just think of the fascinating things you can put into the box—a litter of kittens, three ducks, five puppies, your life savings—in cash! Your dog can help bring home the Christmas presents or help take out the trash. You can give him the chores that no one else wants to do. He won't mind—and everyone else will be ecstatic.

Ideally, you should teach your dog both Tug It and Fetch on Command (Chapter 2) before he learns to drag a box. The trick will be taught from two different approaches, one based on each command.

Start off with a piece of clothesline about two and one half feet long. Knot it so that it forms a circle. If your dog is retrieving on command, throw the rope and tell him to TAKE IT. Do this three or four times with enthusiasm and praise so that Sailor eagerly looks forward to the game. Now take an empty cardboard box, not much higher than your dog's shoulder. Punch a hole in the box, centered and about two inches from the top of the narrow side of the box. Slip the end of the rope opposite the knot through the hole. Now there is a small loop inside the box. Run the knot through the loop and pull it tight. The knot is now hanging outside the box. Now send Sailor to get the rope. As he goes, follow him so that he doesn't have to drag the box too far in order to bring you *the rope*. Give him a lot of encouragement. Begin to move farther and farther away so that Sailor has to drag the box farther and farther to get to you and his praise. If your mood is up, he'll be having a ball and be raring to go when he sees the box. He may even entertain you by fetching the box on his own to entice you to play with him. He may drag it all around and try to fit it through narrow passages where it was

never meant to go. The more you laugh, the more he'll run around with his treasure. Don't worry if it tips over. As we progress, weight will be added to it to keep it upright.

If you have not taught your dog to retrieve or you wish to teach this trick first, take the rope and let him tug on the knot. Most dogs will readily engage in this game of tug-of-war with little prompting. Once this rope becomes a favorite toy of his, you can attach it to the box and let him have a tug-of-war with the box. Gradually add weight to the box by experimenting with different objects. Your dog can be of great assistance at yard-cleaning time by hauling boxes of leaves and branches out to the curb. Getting anyone to help you with your work nowadays is a trick in itself, but adding little creatures to the trick adds greatly to its appeal in a performance. What could be a cuter finale for your act than Sailor dragging out his box full of adorable puppies or charming little kittens? Again, the box can be decorated, he can wear a costume, and this enjoyable game can add a lot of humor and color to any dog act.

WALK ON FOREQUARTERS

This is one of the most difficult of the classic circus tricks. Small dogs are invariably used to do this work. As you read on, you'll readily see why.

Positioning is all important in walking on forequarters. At the first few trials, the dog's hindquarters are held up and the dog is moved in a wheelbarrow fashion. Do not pursue the wheelbarrow position too long, though. The hindquarters must gradually be moved higher and higher over the back so that the forequarters are strengthened and conditioned to carry more and more weight. The hindquarters must be curled up tightly, as in the picture.

They must be tucked up and held over the dog's center of gravity. The dog's center of gravity will shift when he arches his back properly, thus giving him the necessary balance.

The command WALK is given once you help your dog to hold his hindquarters over his back. Your hand should apply gentle pressure forward on the lower part of the hindquarters. This pressure gives the dog a slight forward thrust. Should your charge remain stationary, do not push forward, as this will unbalance him. As long as he is standing, he is learning and conditioning himself to perform this exercise. Expect this to take time. He must build his endurance slowly for this difficult trick. As he works and builds his strength, reward him by gently scratching his stomach without applying any pressure. And don't forget to tell him how swell he is.

When your dog masters this trick, he qualifies as an exceptional trick dog.

Positioning is all important.

"You can do it, baby!" *Pixie La Motte— Long Coat Chihuahua*

You can both be proud. But the technique must be slow, methodical, and persistent. Don't rush. The only time to move along rapidly is when you first elevate the dog's hindquarters off the ground. Get them in that high position as soon as possible. Then have the patience to let your little dog build up strength in his forequarters. This means short, daily practice sessions. The best place to work is on a tabletop. You will have your dog at eye level so that you can make sure he is in the correct position. And it will save you an awful lot of bending, too. What can you do if you love this trick and you own a St. Bernard? Easy! Buy him a Fox Terrier as a friend.

ZIGZAG

The beauty of this trick, a standby for many circus and stage acts, is that there are a number of fine variations that can be done with a good deal less effort than the initial trick. When your dog Zigzags, he simply walks between your legs—one after the other after the other—as you continue to walk. When doing this trick with Sidney, he will be in the Heel position and you must begin to walk on your *right* leg. This will avoid tripping over Sidney. It will also prevent him from getting confused and thinking he should be Heeling.

Sidney is at your left side, wearing his collar and leash. Stretch your right leg as far forward as you can, bend your knees slightly to give Sid some room, and pass the leash under your right leg so that you can lead him under and out toward your right. Command ZIGZAG as you give Sid a gentle tug on the leash to get him moving. Of course, if you are five feet tall and your Sidney is an Irish Wolfhound, this trick might give you quite a jolt.

As Sidney passes under your right leg, step far forward on your left and pass the leash under your left leg to tug him through. Fifteen steps at a session will be sufficient. As you go on, your dog will resist less and less. This cute trick is, after all, rather painless. Once Sid is about eighty per cent on target, you can take the leash off and bait him with small bits of cheese. Step off your right leg, say ZIGZAG, and hold the cheese in your right hand outside your right leg, guiding Sidney under your extended leg. Advance the next leg and guide Sidney under the arch it forms by holding the cheese in your left hand. Then it's simple—right, left, right, left. When Sid is full or your legs are tired, you can knock it off for the day.

Consider your job complete when Sidney will Zigzag without bait. As you wean him off the cheese, begin to make him work for a while before he gets his cheese. But remember that he wants to work for something, so tell him what a good guy he is for a job well done.

The variations on Zigzag are surprisingly flashy. If Sidney knows how to walk on his hindquarters, it will be easy to combine these two tricks. To do

Bend your knees slightly as you step far forward.

Lead him through.

And through again. *Thor Heller—Norwegian Elkhound*

that, though, he will have to be short or you will have to have very long legs. If you can walk on your hands, Sid can Zigzag through your arms instead of your legs. Don't forget to give him a kiss as he passes through. Still another switch is to teach Sidney to Zigzag through another dog's legs. The other dog should be quite large and standing still as Sidney weaves his way through. Other variations? We leave those to your own fertile imagination.

11. Amazing Tricks

From the simplest to the most difficult, these tricks are all show stoppers. They will flabbergast your company or, put together as a theatrical routine, bring down the house. What do our AMAZING TRICKS have in common? You guessed it! They are all amazing.

SPEAK, COUNT, ADD

If your dog will bark on command, you can do some of the most mind-boggling, amusing, and fun tricks with him. Some dogs even manage some marvelous learning on their own once they learn to speak on command. A bright dog may figure out suddenly that his voice has clout with humans—he's known that it has with dogs all along. He may begin to communicate his needs by voice on his own. He might bark to go out, bark near his empty water bowl, or announce other needs and desires. If not, you can help him to do all these things as well as some very fabulous and flashy tricks. You will even learn how to turn this trick to good use for safety and protection. This is not one to miss.

Notice what makes your dog bark—someone at the door, the desire to play with you or another dog, the arrival of the postman or trash collector, the sight of food. Begin by anticipating his bark and telling him to speak just when he is about to give voice anyway. Use the command SPEAK and praise him when he does. Patiently, try this soft method several times a day for a few weeks.

Now hold up a bit of food in front of your dog. Talk to him to excite him, asking, "Do you want this? Do you want this? Speak for the food!" If he barks, give him the treat. As soon as he is barking reliably for the food, change to a hand signal, still baiting him with food. Use a point or a snap.

If you cannot get your dog to bark on command by anticipating his barks

Let him use his fingers if he must.

or by baiting him with food, try one of the two following blockbusters: confine him and let him see you pet another dog, or tie him on a rather short leash at feeding time and place his bowl of food out of reach. In either case, keep telling him to speak and reward him when he does.

Sometimes, when trying to teach a dog to speak on command, you will accidentally start him sneezing instead. If you've missed the chance to invest early in Exxon or AT & T, don't toss away *this* blue chip opportunity. Turn immediately to SNEEZE and teach that first.

Once your dog speaks on voice or hand signal, begin to alternate sessions with food treats and without so that he doesn't become a "food junkie." Dogs are simple creatures and in the presence of food a good part of their concentration is on the food and not on the education. Using food to begin a dog on tricks is fine practice, but if you want real learning to take place, get rid of the treat each time as soon as it is feasible. A dog who works for praise will eventually be working, too, for the love of the work. A dog who works for food will stay at that level and not advance.

Now you are ready to build on your trick. Accustom your dog to speaking from a Sit Front position, alternating all methods: treat, voice command, hand signal, combinations of these. This way you have maximum flexibility for building on this fun trick. Ask your dog any question that can be answered by a number: How old am I? (Be careful. He'll tell.) What's the date? If you're patient, how many states are there in the United States? How long does a United States President serve in office? How many legs does a cow have? Give him the hand signal to begin, but do it subtly so that he sees it but your astounded audience doesn't. If he's having a problem and you're performing, you can always help him along by saying, "Come on. *Speak* up. Tell us how many legs a cow has."

Showmanship

At this point it's only fair to tell you that it will be your job to make your dog look good. After all, he's making you look good. What if he does goof?

What if he doesn't bark or if he gives the wrong answer? He can't ad-lib his way out of the situation, but you can. Your gift of gab can make this good trick look great. If he slurs a bark and is giving the wrong answer, tell him to speak up clearly with full barks or to begin again and get it right. Be prepared to correct him in a way your audience won't spot as a correction. Cover for him—he's your pal. "Didn't you check the calendar today?" "I see you're not up on your history—you forgot Alaska and Hawaii." "You forgot my last two birthdays, you doll." Only your patter can punch this trick up to the limelight it deserves.

Once your dog is responding well, ask him his number question, "How much is two plus five?" and look him squarely in the eyes. When he barks the correct answer, seven (brush up on your math or you're doomed), look away, pause, and praise him. At this point, only a pro will spot the trick in the trick and you are limited only by your own imagination and wit. If you are doing a demonstration or show, you can end with a funny number question such as, "How old am I?" and stop the dog before he barks out the tragic truth by *breaking eye contact* and saying, "I'm afraid we're out of time now."

WALK YOURSELF

This trick sounds like the realization of every dog owner's fantasy. Open the door, send Babe out for her stroll. Perhaps she'll pick up rolls for breakfast and the morning newspaper and then return home. Yes? No! This is not a useful trick. Sorry about that. But it's a darn cute one.

Surely by now you have taught Babe to retrieve, realizing how many snazzy tricks are based on this skill. So she will not object to holding objects in her mouth. Put her collar and leash on her, fold the leash neatly, and tell her BABE, TAKE IT. Place the folded leash, rubber banded if you want to make it easier for her, in her mouth. Now, BABE, HEEL. Practice makes perfect. Even if she is a swell retriever, she may spit it out at first. Try again. Praise her. Keep heeling. Take the leash, saying OUT. Take five. Try it again.

If this isn't cute enough for you (Boy! Are you demanding!), clip the leash to your belt hook and tell her to TAKE IT, offering her the loop. Now your Babe can walk you!

WALK ANOTHER DOG

You hate to get up early, get dressed, and tramp out in the snow with your Irish Water Spaniel, Jack Daniels. So you go out and buy a female, Jill

Daniels. Now, every morning, Jill takes Jack for a walk and you get to sleep late. Nice work if you can get it—but again, this swell trick won't quite accomplish that dream for you. Unless you build a run, or have a very understanding spouse, you'll still have to walk Jack and Jill yourself.

But if you have an unusual flair for comedy, Jack and Jill can walk each other when you're around. Since you have trained Jack to be a super retriever, he will happily take Jill's leash in his mouth and hold it tight. What a pair. What a sight. What a photo.

How is it done? First, Jack and Jill should learn to Heel together, both at your left side. Since you have obedience-trained both of them, this is very little extra work. Have Jack on the outside, since he is a true gentleman. You can buy a brace that will allow each of their choke chains to work when attached to one leash. Or you can slip the leash through the ring of Jill's collar and then clip the snap to Jack's. Or, for a short while, you can use two leashes, which will enable you to correct the dogs separately. Now practice heeling your team of dogs, side by side, a classy "trick" in itself. The compliments will come rolling in. Be sure to praise both the inside and outside dogs when they do their automatic sit. When they are happy with this arrangement, ask Jack to hold Jill's leash and tell them DOGS, HEEL. Now your darling twosome will heel side by side and your hands are free.

You can improvise on this trick, as usual. Jack can hold the leash while Jill performs a Sit, Stand, or Down Stay. We're afraid you still have to be there to call the shots, but we're sure you wouldn't want to miss the fun anyway. If you've taught the dogs other tricks, combine them. Give Jill the leash to hold for a change and tell her to take Jack to "Mommy." With a little practice and humorous fumbling, they should both get there safe and sound. We once had the serendipitous pleasure of bumping into a trained chimp at Bloomingdale's. The chimp took our Golden Retriever's collar and gave him a walk. Our Golden, good-natured slob that he is, went along

with the gag. While you trained *your* dog, he no doubt also learned that the beast who held the leash was boss. So, if a chimp could walk a dog, why not another dog? It may not entirely compensate for getting up early, but it will be a lot of laughs. (If you decide to go big time and get a chimp to walk your dog, be sure he's on roller skates. Our friend was.)

READ

Several out-of-print dog books purport to tell gullible owners how to teach their dogs to read. Cards are made—sort of like the flash cards used in school to teach first-graders how to read. One would say BONE, another might say WATER. In theory, your dog will learn that if he wants his bone he should approach the set of flash cards, read them, pick out the BONE card, and bring it to you. Or he might read and bring the card when you ask him BOSCO, ARE YOU IN THE MOOD FOR A BONE? In fact, can your faithful pooch learn to read? Don't count on it. But if you like to be silly and fool your friends, by all means play school with Bosco and teach him to "read."

Make a few flash cards—BONE, CHEESE, WALK, TREAT. Teach one card at a time. (Notice we didn't say one word at a time.) Keep the flash cards separate and handle them with care. Each card will be rubbed with a specific scent that your dog will associate with the reward you will give him for "reading." First, you can rub a nice, greasy knucklebone on the BONE card. Try to find a color for the card that will not show stains. Or blame the stains on poor Bosco. Next you can impregnate the CHEESE card with the scent of cheese. Remember that your dog's nose is far more efficient than yours. No need to smell up the whole house while doing this trick. The TREAT card can smell like any favorite treat that your dog adores— bologna, chocolate, pizza. (And shame on you! Why is your poor dog eating all that junk food, anyway?) For the WALK card, we can leave this to your fine imagination. Grass, pine scent, old socks—anything associated with a walk will do. Each card should have its own little rack and not be kept in a pack with cards touching each other and scents mingling. Now, one at a time, you can teach your dog the word that goes with each smell. Of course, if you want him to *bring* you the card and not merely go up to it, he must know how to retrieve.

There are several approaches to this trick. The easiest would be to teach it like a variation of SMELL IT—FIND IT! Give your dog the scent of cheese. Tell him BOSCO, FIND THE CHEESE. DO YOU WANT SOME CHEESE? etc. Urge him forward. When he sniffs out the right card, praise him and tell him to TAKE IT. Now back up, calling him to you. Take the card, praise your dog, and give him some C-H-E-E-S-E. With motivation like this, it won't take him long to become an A student.

"Serious, cultured, literate."

Soon you'll be able to line up all four cards in their racks and, by asking the right question, get the right card. By now Bosco has associated the smells with the new words. BOSCO, WHAT GOES WELL WITH HAM? *Voilà!* The CHEESE card. You and your pet ham can astound your guests with an impressive display. Play it your way. Teach him to fetch the CHEESE card on the word HAM. Perhaps he'll fetch the WALK card when you ask WHAT DO WE DO WHEN THE CAR BREAKS DOWN? Since you're being silly, you might as well go all the way.

But what if we are wrong! What if your Fulbright scholar does indeed learn how to read? Well *c'est la vie*. At least have Bosco send us a letter. Any dog that could learn how to read should surely be able to learn how to write—or at least dictate.

FIND THE TEN-DOLLAR BILL

We wish we could tell you that this trick meant sending out little Hester for a walk and having her come home with a ten-dollar bill. Alas, we don't know that trick. Nevertheless, this is a very fine one that we are sure you'll enjoy. At one time, it was done with a dime and a penny. But with inflation, this trick is now done with a single and a ten-dollar bill. It will be Hester's job to find the ten. (Hester has taste. What would she do with a single?)

Get a single and a ten-spot from your audience. A good magician never risks his own dough in a trick—just in case. Now find someone to hold the bills, one in the right hand and one in the left. Make sure that you and Hester can't see which bill is in which hand. Now ask your someone to multiply mentally what is in his right hand by four and what is in the left hand by five. Ask for the total of both numbers. Now you can announce that little Hester will bark three times if the single is in the right hand and five times if the single is in the left hand. Of course, you will be cuing Hester so she will come up with the right answer. Perhaps she'll get the ten as her reward!

The trick is simple. If the answer is even, the single is in the right hand. If it is odd, the single is in the left hand. Don't have Hester bark an odd or an even number as her answer because that might point the spectators toward the secret of your trick.

Now what can you do if your audience cries, "Do it again!" Have someone else try it and multiply the bill in his right hand by four, six, or eight and the bill in his left hand by three, five, or seven. If the total he gives you is even, the single is in the right hand and the ten is in the left. On this performance, pick out the hand with the ten for the sake of variety. Then you can switch to a single and a five. The person holding the money will be told to multiply the bill in his right hand by fourteen and the one in his left hand by—you guessed it—fourteen. Tell him to add the two numbers and give you the total. But in this case, that's just for show. It is easy to multiply one by fourteen. It is more difficult to multiply five by fourteen. So the hand he struggles over has the five-dollar bill. To keep things square with your audience, keep Hester barking three barks for the right hand and five for the left. If possible, write this "code" down at the beginning of your performance. If even one person in the audience feels that the dog mixed up her numbers, the trick loses a lot of its validity. After all, *you* are looking good, but this is a dog trick book!

MARIJUANA DETECTION

This trick is as modern as the growth of the illegal use of marijuana. Whether you want to help out your local police department or have your dog find marijuana for fun and profit, first check the laws in your state. The marijuana laws vary widely from place to place, as do the penalties for illegal possession. Claiming that your stash is on hand merely for the purpose of dog training will not hold water in court. Occasionally, though, you can get co-operation from the local law enforcement agency and it may be possible to get a court order that will permit you to draw marijuana from the police department for this purpose. In this case, you would be "borrowing" marijuana that the police have seized and were holding for evidence. The grass would be carefully weighed in and out every time you needed it to train your dog. But it is difficult to obtain this legal court order. In view of this, how *does* one obtain the marijuana with which to train the dog? We'd advise you to stay away from the friendly neighborhood drug dealer. Everyone knows someone who smokes grass—even if they do not know that they know someone who smokes grass. If you can't get some pot, grass, tea, or reefers this way, go to a rock concert, drop in at the local high school, or merely go to the movies. We're sure you and Popeye will be able to get to work now.

The Knowing Nose

We can put a man on the moon, but we are unable to come up with a device that can measure the olfactory acuity of the dog. Our equipment is far too primitive in comparison to the nose of a dog. It is this ability to smell infinitesimally minute odors that enables the dog to sniff out marijuana. To get an idea of how powerful your canine friend's sense of smell really is, sniff around the following facts:

Dogs can smell a man two hundred yards away.
Dogs can detect salt diluted one hundred thousand times.
Dogs can tell both the difference and similarity between identical twins by smelling.
Dogs can smell a bird seventy-five yards away.
Dogs can detect sulfuric acid diluted one million times.
Dogs can tell the difference and similarity between a person's odor at different parts of the body (e.g., palm vs. armpit)
It is impossible to mask an odor from a dog.
Dogs can smell odors through "airtight" containers.

These facts cannot be tested or proved with scientific instruments. They can only be demonstrated by training dogs to accomplish these tasks.

The Four Methods of Training

1. NATURAL RETRIEVING METHOD. With a natural retriever, motivation is easy to instill and the work will be easier to teach. The United States Government requires all marijuana dogs to be natural retrievers.

2. FORCED RETRIEVING METHOD. This type of training indicates a greater degree of dependability, but the training itself is much harder. Methods 1 and 2 have been discussed earlier (see Fetch on Command, in Chapter 2).

3. AGITATION METHOD. In this method, a dog is first taught to attack on command. He is then agitated by a man who always has the aroma of marijuana on his clothes. The sack that the dog will bite into will have grass bound up in it. If the dog is aggressive and if he enjoys the attack work, he will become a fast-working, well-motivated marijuana dog. However, this type of training is ill suited for all but military work. These dogs are very aggressive. Less control than usual is used during their training in order to increase their drive to locate marijuana. Only in a military setting where the movement of the soldiers is entirely under control is this dog a safe bet. If a dog such as this were used around civilians, their safety would be threatened.

4. FOOD REWARD METHOD. This is a difficult technique for teaching marijuana detection. In the initial stages of training, small bits of cheese are placed on top of the marijuana. The dog is attracted to the cheese, and in the beginning of the training he is allowed to eat it. As training and skill progress, he must locate the marijuana and cheese and sit before he takes the cheese. Next, the trainer will remove the cheese and feed it to the dog by hand as his reward for the find. A dog trained in this way alerts in an unusual manner. He not only sits but he turns his head slightly up and toward his handler to receive his food reward. While this is an easy alert to read, it is rather difficult to develop real drive in these dogs. The method is used only when there is fear that the marijuana will be booby-trapped. A similar technique is used in training explosive-detector dogs.

Handling the Grass and Training the Dog

It takes a pound of grass to properly train a good marijuana dog. If you plan to use this "trick" just for your own fun, you can get away with a smaller amount of the stuff. The reason for the ample supply is that you cannot use the same marijuana over and over again. Familiar odors will build up and the dog will begin to work off these odors rather than the marijuana odor. You'll have to use different grass in different containers during the training. The amount of precision and care you put into the training depends upon your goal.

Begin with a two-ounce stash and put it into an old but freshly laundered sock. Tie a knot in the sock to prevent the marijuana from falling out, though, of course, there will be a little loss through the fabric. Toss the sock up in the air and encourage Popeye's interest. Motivation is highly important in this work. Now toss it for him to catch or fetch. Don't worry about a precision retrieve. We are only interested in developing the dog's drive for finding marijuana. We are not getting him ready for the obedience ring. Work with Popeye for short sessions. Unless he's really into it, three retrieves at a session will be plenty for a start. Play this as a game. We want Popeye to get excited and jump around when he sees the sock. If he begins to fade, stop the game.

Playtime! Toss the sock, telling Popeye FIND THE GRASS. When he brings it back, praise him warmly. Don't worry if he won't give it up right away. Let him get excited and enjoy the game. Let his nose work. The background information you might need to help you will be found in Fetch on Command in Chapter 2 and in Smell It—Find It! (Chapter 3). Now you're both cooking with gas! Popeye is interested in the sock and the game and the praise. You are interested in a dog who will help you to find marijuana. Now you can begin to hide the sock and have Popeye find it. Don't make it too rough on him. Remember that you want him to succeed. The search will gradually become more and more difficult as his skill and motivation both increase. Hide the sock at first so that a piece of it is sticking out from the hiding place. Next, to make sure he is not using his eyes, hide the sock under an upholstered chair. Encourage him as he sniffs for it, but do not become anxious if he takes a few minutes. As long as he is working and interested, you are on the right track.

Now that Popeye is working well on the sock, you will have to make his task a little harder. Buy some sandwich bags that "lock the flavor and freshness in." Put two ounces of fresh marijuana in one of the bags and let it sit overnight in a hiding place. First thing in the morning, work Popeye on finding the marijuana. He should locate it with ease. So much for airtight containers.

After Popeye retrieves the marijuana a few times, you will notice some small holes in the plastic bag. Simply put the bag of marijuana inside an-

other plastic bag—and add a new bag over the old whenever the old gets raggedy. Letting the marijuana sit in a hiding spot overnight makes Popeye's work much easier. You want him to succeed and you're going to help him do just that. But gradually the job will have to be made more difficult. As you do this, always praise him well for a find, never, never let him quit without finding the marijuana, work him for longer and longer periods of time and work him on smaller and smaller amounts of grass. Less grass means less odor for Popeye to work from—so help him, but not all the time. To prevent his quitting without success, you may sometimes have to guide him to where he can smell the marijuana. Only do this if he seems bored and likely to quit. Otherwise, patience is the key word.

Popeye should learn to find marijuana in all sorts of containers because you never know how it will be stored. The variety of marijuana containers is endless. A metal Band-Aid container is commonly referred to as a lid when it is stuffed with marijuana. Airtight and waterproof 35 mm camera film containers make excellent places to store marijuana. When working Popeye on any airtight container, you must let it sit for a while to let the odor seep through. If you work him immediately, he will be unsuccessful. In fact, if you try him without letting the canister sit and he *does* find it, it probably means that you were careless in filling it and left a marijuana residue on the outside of the container. The first time you run your dog on an airtight container, let it sit for a twenty-four-hour period. A fairly good grass dog can find the marijuana after about six hours. So if you work Popeye up to this standard, you've got a grass dog to be proud of.

If you are working along with Popeye and both loving it, you may be going broke from buying all that marijuana. Occasionally, for an economic break, you can use the seeds and twigs of the marijuana which are not suitable for smoking and are discarded. This material *is* suitable, however, for teaching a dog to locate marijuana.

In marijuana-detection training, search techniques are extremely important. You and your dog must learn to divide a room in a logical manner and follow a pattern that will enable you to cover the entire room without missing anything. You do not want your dog sniffing around aimlessly and getting bored. Work the walls first. Then work the center of the room. At first, Popeye went alone to find the marijuana. His pattern was erratic. Now you can put him on leash, using a flat leather collar and giving him the command in a low, whispering tone of voice—FIND THE GRASS, WHERE'S THE GRASS? Now you will be able to guide Popeye in his search. Be sure to cover any of the logical areas where marijuana is likely to be hidden.

Once your dog excels at room searches, start him on body searches. First hide some marijuana near a person. Ultimately hide the marijuana in pockets, clothing, belt buckles, etc. But don't rush your dog into finding grass on a person. It might confuse him if you try this too soon.

Shortly after your first training-playing sessions with grass in a sock, Popeye will be looking for marijuana as eagerly as the most confirmed "head." Now you can use Popeye with the utmost confidence. Happy hunting.

12. Magic Tricks, Sleight of Paw, Card Tricks

Since the beginning of time, magic has appealed to kids of all ages. A good magic trick or flashy card trick will turn any octogenarian into a starry-eyed kid again. But can dogs perform feats of magic? You bet they can! The paw is quicker than the eye—and, believe it or not, your dog *does* have something up his sleeve.

CARD IN THE HANDKERCHIEF

This is a simple trick that can be done with a minimum amount of practice *once your dog is a reliable retriever*. Present a deck of fanned-out cards to your audience and ask someone to pick a card. "Don't let me see it. Make sure that the dog doesn't see it!" The last sentence adds a little humor to the act, particularly if the dog is just wandering around aimlessly. The person selecting the card will make an attempt to hide the card from the dog. Have the person return the card to the deck and shuffle the deck. Ask the person who took the card to drape a large handkerchief over your hands, cards and all. Now say, "Merlin, take the handkerchief!"

Under the handkerchief, hidden from your audience, Merlin is receiving a little help from his best friend. You are using a "stripper deck," which can be purchased at a local magic or novelty shop. A stripper deck is one in which all the cards are minutely tapered to one end. After the person selects a card, close the fanned deck and turn it around in the other direction. As the selected card is returned to the deck, it will be the only card tapered in the opposite direction. Once the handkerchief is placed over your hands, the thumb and forefinger of one hand simply run along the sides of the deck. The right card is then slid out of the deck, under cover of the handkerchief, and presented to the dog inside the handkerchief.

"Voilà! The correct card is in the handkerchief." *Sheba Koehler, C.D.X.—Collie*

In the initial phases of practicing this trick, the dog may be confused. Repeat the command TAKE IT while holding the handkerchief directly in front of the dog. Your job will be much easier if you have had Merlin retrieve handkerchiefs, silks, and other types of cloth. After Merlin has seized the handkerchief with the correct card in it (unbeknownst to your spectators), tell him to take the card to the pretty lady who selected it (see Carry a Message, in Chapter 3). It will look like the dog is carrying only the handkerchief, but, *voilà!* Inside is the correct card.

SHELL GAME

The shell game is a classic con game that looks good on an innocent dog.

You have an object, let's say it's a dog biscuit, and you have three plastic cups or three small plastic flowerpots. Put the Amazing Kreskin on a Sit Stay. Place the biscuit on the floor and cover it with an inverted cup. Now invert the two other cups and place them all in a row. Tell Kreskin to watch your hands carefully. Now slide the cups around rapidly, making sure the biscuit slides with the cup it's under. When the cups are realigned, tell Kreskin FIND IT. (Refer to Smell It—Find It! in Chapter 3, for prerequisite training.) Kreskin will knock over the cup with his nose, *voilà!* a snack. Once Kreskin is on to the game, you can change the hiding object. Now play with a marble or a golf ball. Will he find it? Place your bets, folks. As usual, our money is on the dog. The hand may be quicker than the eye, but it's never quicker than the nose.

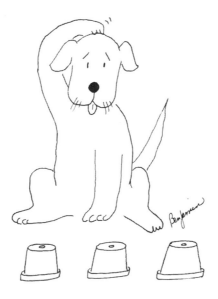

"Where did it go?"

MAGIC NUMBERS

In any counting trick, try to keep your answers lower than ten and higher than two. Two things happen when you go over ten. Your audience may lose count and your dog will become bored and impatient. If you have a lot of answers, on the other hand, that are *one*, you will have to cut your dog short just as he is getting going. If you do this enough times, he will become hesitant in his counting. This doesn't mean that you can *never* use one as an answer. Just keep it to a minimum.

Good manners among magicians dictate that you never reveal the secret behind a trick to your audience. Revealing the secret erases all the enchantment—and that's what your audience is there for. Instead, enhance the enchantment with your "patter." Patter, as you know, is what you say while you and your dog are performing. It is lighthearted talk. It often endears both you and your dog to your audience. It adds humor. It is a way to cover when you make a mistake or your dog does. And you can be sure of this. If you perform enough, you will both goof. A witty tongue and a smooth and relaxed patter are the best friends a performer can have.

Ask your audience to "Think of a number, any number, but don't tell me what it is. Please write it down but don't let Mandrake see what you are writing. That's right. Cover your answer. Now add that number to the next higher one in sequence. Add nine to the total. Now divide by two. Now subtract the original number from the total." Turn to Mandrake and get his attention. If he is busy with his fleas, promise him a pay cut. Now you can cue him to bark five times. Your audience is amazed. The dog is correct. And he didn't even have pencil and paper. Don't say you heard it here, but there's no magic involved. The answer is always five! Now your audience pleads, "Do it again. Do it again." With the answer being always five, that would be suicide. So you will, of course, vary the trick.

Instead of telling your audience to add nine to their number, choose another odd number. If you keep the same sequence of instruction in your patter, you will come up with a different answer. Also, please add a joke or two, for variety. If they add seven, the answer will be four. If they add eleven, the answer will be six. Even Mandrake knows that! The code is as follows: add one to the odd number given and divide by two for the correct answer. Here is what the formula looks like:

Add:	3	5	7	9	11	13	15	17	19
Answ.	2	3	4	5	6	7	8	9	10

Remember—try not to go over ten barks. And you have an audience, babe, so have those jokes and funny stories ready.

THE LOST DIGIT

Once your stage presence is developed, you can move into this delightful trick. You and your dog Albert, the Mathematical Marvel, are going to help your friend locate a lost digit. Tell your friend, "Write down any four-figure number. Don't let me see it. Don't let Albert see the number!" Your friend writes down 2468. Now say, "Kindly add up all four digits. It's okay to use your fingers, but don't let Albert watch you count." Your friend's total is 20. "Now cross out any one of the original four digits." Your friend crosses out the second digit, a four. Ask your friend to "Write the three digits that are left over above the total of the four digits and subtract the total from your three-digit number." Your friend subtracts 20 from 268 and gets 248. "Tell Albert the total." Your friend will tell Albert that his total is 248. Now you can ask Albert for the answer—what is the lost digit—and he will bark four times.

As soon as you get that last answer from your friend, add up those digits, which will give you a total of fourteen. Deduct fourteen from the nearest multiple of nine, which in this case is nine times two, or eighteen. The answer you get is—four—the lost digit. Try it with any four-digit number and you will see that it works!

But—what if the answer works out to be either nine or eighteen? Here is where your newly acquired stage presence will come in handy. In this case, the answer is either nine or zero. And you have no way of telling. Wheel around to Albert, stare him squarely in the face and demand, "What's the answer?" Your startled dog will do a double take. He is not used to this kind of treatment. Whirl back to your friend, saying, "It's not a zero, is it? Albert can't bark a zero." If you are told that it *is* a zero, lavish praise upon Albert. After all, you just startled the heck out of him. "Albert, you're terrific. I never knew you could answer a question with a zero answer!" If your friend says it is not a zero, then you know it is a nine. Now you can turn back to Albert and apologize for not giving him enough time to answer. Albert will bark on your cue and, with a little help from his friend, stop at nine, the clever little over achiever!

13. Tricks Are for Kids

Since everyone agrees that dogs and kids are a natural, these tricks have been designed to entertain and educate the younger set. With these under your belt, both you and your dog will be heroes in your child's eyes.

SPELLING TRICKS

This is a simple but flashy trick that will make your dog look smarter than he is and may help motivate your child to put in a little more time on homework. It can be approached from several paths.

You can teach your dog a basic spelling trick directly without previous training. Put a collar and leash on your dog and spell out S-I-T. As you do, pull up on his leash and push down on his rump. Behold a miracle! Now praise him for his sit. Or praise him for his S-I-T. In this way, he is merely learning to respond to S-I-T instead of the word SIT. Repeat as often as is necessary for him to respond without help from you.

If your dog knows the command SIT, you can teach him to respond and sit to a hand signal. As you say SIT, hold your hand with the palm up and curl up your fingers. After a few practice sessions, you can drop the voice command and he will sit when he sees the hand signal. Now take him to the next step by curling your hand up as you spell S-I-T. Once he has had some practice with this, drop the hand signal and he will sit when you spell his command.

If you wish to make a good trick better, do not let your dog anticipate your good spelling. If he sits when he hears the letter *S,* correct him gently and make him wait for you to spell out S-I-T. Now try misspelling SIT. When you spell S-A-T or S-I-T-E, he should not sit. If he does, tell him NO. Then spell SIT correctly and praise him for sitting.

Patient practice will get him to respond to any number of commands when you spell them. Children (as well as adults) will be amazed at his advanced schooling. You can add some flair by saying, "Do you think Sam can find his B-O-N-E?" Build the trick using your own inimitable style.

RING AROUND THE ROSY

This is a very special game for very special people—little kids. Since you have obedience-trained your dog and he knows the command DOWN, half your work is already done! Lucky you. Take your Irish Wolfhounds, Nora and Padrick, into your living room and put them on leash. Walk in front of them and call them to follow you. If they try to Heel, gently guide them behind you with the leash, telling them NO, FOLLOW. Walk in a large circle. Praise them as you go. Practice this for a few minutes at a time, twice a day.

After a week, have Nora and Padrick begin to follow you in a circle off leash. If they balk, work with their leashes on a few more times. Now have another adult walk the circle, too, and have the dogs follow. Once they can do this, bring on the children and start the song:

Ring around the Rosey,
A pocket full of Posies.
Ashes, ashes,
All fall down.

When the kids get to "All fall down," have them emphasize the word DOWN and fall down themselves. Give the kids and the Wolfhounds some big praise. Now you can have fun with this game whenever you have a couple of Irish Wolfhounds and a couple of kids around the house. But don't do it too many times in a row or both your dogs and your little kids will get dizzy.

"All fall down." *Nora and Padrick McIntosh—Irish Wolfhounds*

JUMP ROPE

No doubt about it—this is a tough trick. There are a number of ways to teach this trick, but the method we prefer is getting the dog up on a box. The box should be steady and large enough for the dog to turn around on, but not so large as to permit him to wander around. The box will thus confine him to a small work area. A stick is introduced and slowly slid under his feet. If your dog walks on his hindquarters, slowly slip the stick under one foot and then the other. If he is working on all fours, slide the stick under the forequarters first and then the hindquarters. At first, proceed slowly so that the dog can step over the stick, which slides a fraction of an inch above the surface of the box. Then, increase the tempo and rotate the stick around the back of the dog. Don't rush—this work will take quite a while.

Initially your sessions will be short, a minute or two at a time. They are slowly increased to ten minutes. A dog must develop endurance for this type of work. Some dogs will pick up the *idea* very quickly and others will take a long time to figure out what is happening. When your dog has the idea, the co-ordination, and the endurance to do this trick, substitute a rope for the stick. The box controlled his movement. The stick gave him a rigid object to jump over. Now he's ready to get off the box and jump rope. Try him a few times to make sure he's learned his lesson well. And now that you've done all this hard work, your kids get to have the fun of jumping rope with their dog. They probably still won't write you after they grow up and move away from home—but at least you can get some great pictures to remember them by.

HIDE-AND-SEEK

If your dog is to be a proper playmate for a child, he should learn how to play HIDE-AND-SEEK thoroughly. He should, of course, learn how to hide and wait until he is found. He should also learn to hide his eyes while your child finds a hiding place and then do the finding. Be careful on the second part. We've seen dogs peek.

Have your child help you teach this trick to Snoopy. Let her hide her eyes and count while you escort Snoopy to his hiding place, let's say in a closet. Have Snoopy lie down in the back of the closet and STAY. Now tell Laurie to find Snoopy. If, during the training, Snoopy breaks, correct him and put him back in his hiding place on a STAY. When Laurie does find him, she can tell him OKAY and give him a treat. Then, of course, he can and will leave his hiding place.

Each time you play, tell Snoopy GO AND HIDE and lead him to a hiding place, a different one each time. Give him enough variety of places so that he can play the game well. And always give him lots of praise for any step he does on his own. After a few weeks, you will be able to tell him SNOOPY, GO AND HIDE. If necessary, you can just point the way to one of his hiding places while Laurie is counting.

Once Snoopy is a master hider, it's only fair to teach him to seek, too. The position he needs for his "counting" is the same as for SAY YOUR PRAYERS (in Chapter 4). Just tell him PAWS UP, HIDE YOUR EYES, and you count. Of course, your dog can count himself (see Speak, Count, Add, in Chapter 11). But getting him to count *and* hide his eyes would be a bit much. He'll also have trouble counting by fives! After you count and say READY OR NOT HERE COMES SNOOPY, tell Snoopy FIND LAURIE (see Find a Person, in Chapter 3). Now Snoopy can find Laurie and give *her* a treat—the treat of playing Hide-and-Seek with her dog.

14. New Tricks for Old Dogs

The question is often asked, "Can an old dog learn new tricks?" Common sense will tell you the answer. We'll even bet that *you*'ve learned a thing or two lately, you old dog. Your old dog is now settled down, mellow, and easy to live with. He's probably also bored silly. Begin here and then try him on other tricks, too. All the attention may even make him feel young again.

BRING THE VITAMIN E, GERITOL, OR HEATING PAD

While we've never seen an old dog retire to a rocking chair, this trick will amuse your friends because it involves your old dog in some of the other stereotyped trappings of human old age. Naturally, to get your dog to bring anything, you have had to teach him to retrieve. If you have practiced him as suggested on many objects (see Fetch on Command, in Chapter 2), he is well on his way to accomplishing this new trick for his golden years.

Prepare a small bottle of Vitamin E by wrapping masking tape around the middle so that your dog can pick it up more easily. Toss the bottle and tell Mimi TAKE IT, BRING THE VITAMIN E. After a few practice shots, you can set the taped bottle in an area your old dog can reach, and always keep it there. Now you can send her to fetch her vitamins without a warm-up toss.

Proceed as above with a small bottle of Geritol, taped for convenience in carrying. For safety, take your Geritol every day. No, we're not trying to make you stronger. We just want to avoid a messy spill. Do the trick once your bottle is empty.

Wrap the cord of the heating pad up small and tape it so that it doesn't unravel and drag all over the floor. Begin as above, with a warm-up toss, and then show your dog the spot you have chosen for her prop. Then when company comes, you can say, "I think it's a bit chilly for old Mimi. Mimi, BRING YOUR HEATING PAD." How much is this trick worth to you? It all depends on how much you like to laugh. And what's it worth to Mimi? She won't be likely to plug the heating pad in and lay it across her arthritic knees, but she'll adore being the center of attention again. She may even feel as if she asked you for the moon and you got it for her!

PLAY THE PIANO

This trick is best done with a toy piano. Real pianos are too valuable to let them get scratched up by a dog's nails. Besides, your old dog will look like a "swell" with her toy grand and miniature candelabrum.

Gently seat old Becky in front of her piano. Pat the little keys and tell her PAWS UP, lifting her paws to the keyboard if necessary. Encourage her and reassure her. She'll love the attention, our venerable musician, but the dignity of her age requires gentle handling. Now tell her BECKY, PLAY THE PIANO and, scratching and petting under one foreleg and then the other, help her to alternate paws as she "plays" the piano. Work with old Becky for a few minutes each day until she will easily sit at her piano and bang away at the keys, one paw at a time.

Will the noise bother your neighbors? Not likely. They'll probably assume that your kids have started piano lessons again.

Have him stick to the classics.

15. Emergency Tricks

These "tricks" are more than useful. They explore the depths of a dog's intelligence and of his willingness to serve his master. If you saw these feats performed in a movie, you'd find them amazing. But they are not merely entertaining. They have real clout. Teach them to your dog and hope you never need them.

FIRE AND SMOKE DETECTION

Both time-consuming and troublesome, this trick is the most rewarding in our whole bag of tricks. It can save your life if you should ever need it.

Your dog will have to learn that all fire isn't bad. He will come into contact with fire throughout his life and he just can't bark at it indiscriminately. He mustn't bark when the stove is turned on or when he sees flame in the furnace. He shouldn't bark when you light a fire in the fireplace or every time someone lights a cigarette. Your attitude while conducting his training should be firm and serious. It will never be considered humorous for him to bark at the wrong time or not to bark when he should. And *none* of this training should be done in front of children or put on display in any way. Fire is deadly serious. It isn't a game.

Sterno, or canned heat, produces a small, safe, controlled flame and is a good device to use when teaching a dog smoke and fire detection. Open the can, set the top on the floor, drop a match into the can and call your dog. Point to the Sterno and tell your dog to SPEAK! Praise him when he does. This is enough for the first lesson. To put out the fire, drop the lid back on the can and press it shut with the heel of your shoe. (Obviously, the can will be hot.)

Use the Sterno for short training sessions in different areas of the house and on erratic schedules. Once your dog is barking as soon as he sees the

fire jumping out of the can, you are well on your way. However, make sure
you repeat the exercise at least another dozen times, beginning to intersperse
lit cans with *unlit* ones. The dog should not be learning to bark at Sterno
cans. If he barks at the unlit can, a low but firm NO will stop him. Then
praise him.

While your dog is learning to warn you of fire with his voice, he must also
learn not to bark at controlled fire. Reprimand him with NO for barking at
the fireplace or stove. When he begins to bark at your pipe lighter, softly
correct him with a caress on the shoulder and a gentle NO. When he stops
barking, tell him, "That's a good boy," so that he knows he is doing the right
thing. Remember that the more often you correct him for barking at fire, the
more often you will have to praise him for finding "dangerous" fire or
smoke. He will need a certain amount of follow-up from time to time to as-
sure good retention.

Once your dog barks at the small fire in the Sterno can, occasionally light
and use a tightly rolled-up piece of newspaper, thrust *carefully* in his direction to get him to bark. Be careful, too, of where you work. A linoleum or
concrete floor would be a safer bet than a shag rug. Aim for a continuous
sustained bark rather than a single WOOF. He should persist until the flame
is extinguished. Praise him, initially, *while* he is barking. As you progress,
praise him *after* he has barked for a longer and longer period of time. A single WOOF will not wake you in the middle of the night. However, don't
knock your dog out. Vary long and short sessions so that you build the time
he is able to bark. Try not to bore or overtire your dog with too many long
sessions.

Continue to vary your dog's experience with fire, using Sterno, rolled
newspaper, or a small, controlled fire outdoors. Begin to teach Rover to
bark when you are not around. Set up a Sterno can in a room that is between you and the dog. Call him to come to you so that he will have to pass
the lit can. If you have prepared him sufficiently, he should start barking
when he sees the flame. If he doesn't, bring him back into the room with the

lit Sterno and show it to him. If he barks, rush to him with profuse, warm praise. Always praise him highly when he achieves a new level of success such as barking to attract your attention when you are not in the presence of the fire. Well done.

Smoke Gets in Your Eyes

"Where there's smoke there's fire" is not necessarily true. But if there's a smoke condition in your house, you'll want to know about it. Smoke is more difficult to work with initially, but since you have given your dog a good grounding already, this phase of his training should go faster. Do most of this work out of doors to prevent smoke inhalation and damage to your house. If you live in the country, leaf-raking time will be ideal for this work. Damp leaves are an excellent source of smoke—so excellent that you had best notify the local fire department of your work beforehand. When working indoors, make sure the area is well ventilated. Damp leaves work well indoors, too. For the city dweller, oily rags are a good substitute. But NEVER use gasoline-soaked rags, as they are far too dangerous. Place your leaves or rags in a metal bucket and have a good supply of water standing by. Don't use a metal wastebasket, as it will leak when you put the fire out. Use the same techniques that you used in teaching Rover to bark at fire.

Plan to work for three to six months on this "trick." You may be teaching other exercises at the same time but not during the same sessions. Why spend all this time teaching a dog to detect smoke and fire when there are inexpensive devices on the market to do the job? Fire and smoke detectors are mechanical, and even if they are placed strategically throughout the house, much can go wrong. Dogs are not mechanical devices. We'd put our money on the dog. If you want to play it safest, use both. Could it hurt?

And since this is not a game, proud as you are after all your hard work, low-key your bragging. When someone tells you about the dog who saved an entire family and then ran back into the flames only to emerge later with the fire insurance policy in his mouth, smile. If someone should ask you how to do this dog trick, tell him that every time his house burns down to tell his dog to SPEAK. Better yet, buy him a copy of this book!

UNTIE HANDS—CHEW A ROPE LOOSE

In the movies of days gone by, the hero used to save the heroine who had been tied to the railroad tracks by some wicked blackguard. In the nick of time, just as the train was rapidly approaching down the tracks, our hero would untie the girl and be rewarded with a kiss. Just in case wicked blackguards still exist, and take our word for it—they do, you had better teach your Hero this trick.

"Hurry! Chew!"

"My Hero!" *Miss Crunch—American (Pit) Bull Terrier*

Imagine yourself tied to the tracks. The train is approaching and you can feel the ground beneath you shaking. You call out to your faithful hound, HERO, UNTIE! He releases you in time—and in the background you hear, "Curses, foiled again." You can teach Hero this trick in two different ways—the hard way and the easy way. Teach him both—the easy way first. Don't be lazy. You just never know when it will come in handy.

In the first case, your blackguard isn't very bright and he tied you neatly with a bow, leaving the two loose ends hanging free. This trick then becomes a switch on the TUG IT exercise (in Chapter 17). Hero grabs a loose end of the string and tugs. As bows do, it comes untied and you are free. Simple but impressive in anyone's league.

Now let's suppose that your particular mugger is too smart to tie you up in ribbons and bows. Start Hero off on the string used to hold your roast together. Eating all those roasts will give you the strength to teach Hero this trick—and the savory string will give Hero the initial incentive to learn his new trick. Put Hero in the Sit Front position. Put the flavor-soaked string in his mouth, way in the back on his molars. (These are the grinding teeth three or four teeth behind his fangs.) Laying the cord across his molars, say CHEW! He's no dope. He'll chew. Let him get all the way through the string and give him lots of praise. He'll enjoy the praise almost as much as he enjoyed chewing on the string. But be careful not to let him eat the string. Try him with another flavorful piece of string and the command CHEW! Praise him and knock off work for the day. Gradually work on thicker string, soaking the center in gravy first. Keep up the good work until he can chew through a clothesline. The moment he chews through, reward him energetically. When he is doing a great job on the rope, start holding it behind your back. Now bring on those muggers, thugs, and blackguards. You and Hero are ready for anything.

BARK AT INTRUDERS

There is a difference between a dog that is taught to bark on command and a dog that barks at intruders. In the first instance, the dog is merely barking on cue. In the second, the dog's protective instincts are coming to the fore and his *tone* will be very different. The material covered in SPEAK, COUNT, ADD (in Chapter 11) will help you understand how to teach a dog to bark at intruders. Indeed, the professional trainer often has to use some of these techniques to teach the less protective dog to bark at intruders. Barking on cue is an amusing trick. Barking at intruders is no laughing matter. This trick may save your life. In itself, this exercise is not dangerous as long as it is taught with the proper control and restraint on the part of both dog and owner.

Most dogs should be able to learn to bark at intruders by eighteen months of age. Some of the giant breeds such as St. Bernards and Newfoundlands really do not come into their own until two and a half years of age. A good obedience foundation is essential not only from a control point of view, but also from the point of view of the dog's maturity and awareness of things around him. He must have a wide variety of experience in order to have the confidence to do this type of work well. Too many owners try to push their dogs into this work too early. If your dog lacks the age and confidence for this work, don't push him into it or you can ruin him. You will also note among our caveats that you are required to use an agitator to teach your dog to bark at intruders. Never under any circumstances should you attempt to agitate your own dog or have any member of your family do it.

To start this type of training, you must enlist the aid of someone not known to your dog. Your best choice would be someone who really knows dogs and has had a lot of experience with them. If you can't find a *good* dog expert, find yourself an actor. Now you can make an inventory of your dog's behavior patterns and find out what makes him bark. This may give you some needed short cuts in the training. Assuming that Galahad does not normally bark at "strangers," you can take him out for a walk. Keep him on leash and use a snug, flat leather collar rather than a choke chain. You will cross paths with your actor friend, who will be wearing a slouch hat and a jacket with the collar turned up. He will slink behind a tree. As you approach, the actor will peer out from behind a tree. He can even be wearing a Halloween mask with the eyes enlarged so that his view is not obscured. He should appear as sinister as possible and never stand in a normal fashion. Observe Galahad's reaction. As soon as he spots the "intruder," say in a low voice WHO'S THAT? WATCH 'IM. WHO'S THERE? WATCH 'IM! Your voice should be loaded with suspicion. Should Galahad bark, the intruder will rapidly retreat behind the tree and you will praise Galahad to the skies for protecting you from imminent death. Remember that you are acting too. Don't confuse your dog by doing this work with a smile on your face. Now change your direction so that you do not pass the agitator again. All three of you have done enough work for today.

If Galahad backed up or hid behind your leg, your job will be a little tougher but not impossible. This is where good acting really pays off. At first sign of a whimper or a bark, the agitator will retreat. He looks for an opportunity to withdraw. The dog must be the winner. The dog must do something to frighten off the agitator. If the response is poor, the actor can retreat a good distance to another tree and wait for your approach again. This time the whimper followed by a low woo-oof will be a little faster in coming and your praise will be more exuberant. But do not push the dog too far on his first outing. If results aren't obtained on this first try, it may be advisable to wait until your dog is a little older.

Set up many short sessions—the shorter and more frequent the better. Long sessions can be nerve-shattering to a dog. To Galahad, this is the real thing! Impatience will not get him trained. On the next session, follow the

The agitator will pop out from behind a tree.

same procedure. This time, the agitator comes out from behind the tree a little farther. The dog's barks increase. Now Galahad can actually chase off
the bad guy, who runs out of sight and hides behind another tree on the pre-
arranged route. Gradually increase the length of time of each session.
Galahad is developing a great sense of courage and pride. He knows that the
villain is terrified of him. He starts to bark much faster now. In our next session, the agitator will raise his hand when he comes out. If Galahad flinches
at all, the hand is immediately dropped. Soft-pedal the raised hand and in-
tegrate it into the sessions until the intruder can hold it well above his head
as your dog barks protectively.

You and Galahad are sitting quietly at home. The villain rings your doorbell—or, better still, he fiddles around with the doorknob. Take Galahad by
his collar and lead him to the door. WATCH 'IM is the command and
Galahad frightens off the agitator. Up until this point, you have been ex-
ercising physical control over Galahad. Part of the psychology behind this is
that the restrained dog, like the restrained drunk in a barroom brawl, feels,
"Hold me back or I'll kill 'im." The restraint encourages! Should your dog
be like the cowardly lion, it will make sure that he doesn't "split" when the
bad guy appears for the first time. In the case of the more aggressive dog, it
minimizes the risk of having your assistant bitten.

But by now Galahad is barking and even lunging at the intruder. Now he
needs some additional control. The command OUT, spoken in a short,
crisp, and fairly loud voice, turns off your dog. He once again becomes a
docile pet. If he persists in barking, a jerk on the leash accompanies the word
OUT! If he seems wild and aggressive still, substitute a metal choke collar

for the flat leather collar you have been using and give him a sharper jerk that he certainly will feel. Of course, when you give the command OUT, it goes without saying that the agitator must immediately cease all aggressive activity toward you and Galahad.

OUT is not a correction. The word NO tells the dog he is doing something wrong. OUT means: What you were doing was correct, but I have now changed my mind—so stop. In other words, NO is used to stop behavior you never want your dog to do, and OUT means stop for now.

It matters little whether Galahad is protecting you or himself, as long as he barks when appropriate and stops on command. You are a team and have worked together for the desired results. You have given one another courage. Many owners would like to believe that their dogs would be ready to lay down their lives to protect them. With this trick under Galahad's collar, you will probably never have to put your dog to the test.

FIND A LOST OBJECT

This trick is useful for all dog owners, especially those who keep losing things. There are even dogs that are trained expressly for finding lost items, even if not lost by their owners.

Take Spot to some tall grass and play catch with him. (Of course, he already knows how to retrieve.) Toss an object and let Spot see where it lands. Send him for it. Toss it out a few more times. This is all a game for Spot and he's having the time of his life. Now toss it out and don't let him see where it goes. An eyeglass case or an old glove would be a suitable object to begin with. Again, send Spot to find the glove. Talk him into the area if necessary. Your encouragement is very important. Tell him FIND IT, GOOD BOY, FIND IT, THAT'S MY GOOD BOY. Now he's getting the idea. The energy you give him with your encouraging patter will keep him motivated and on the track. Now you can try heeling with the glove behind your back. Do not let Spot know where you drop the item. When you get some distance from the drop, send Spot to find it. Each time you try this, make the find a little more difficult.

The purpose of the grass is to make it difficult for Spot to spot the glove. When you are working on grass, he also will not be able to hear where you drop the item. Once Spot is working well in high grass and enjoying this new game, change your training area to the street. There he'll have to overcome a lot of new distractions, strange scents, people passing, and noise. This will be a real challenge for your dog and he'll be proud and pleased to rise to the occasion. Besides, there's no guarantee that you'll lose your car keys in tall grass.

At first, stick with the same item. Once he's on to this trick, you can change to something new. From then on, vary the object to be found. The next time you lose your keys or glasses, you will realize that this special trick is worth the little bit of effort it takes to teach it. But do be sure that when you lose something of value Spot is with you.

Working in the grass forces Spot to use his nose.

FOOD REFUSAL

There are countless variations on food refusal, all of which make impressive tricks. But trick or not, this work could save your dog's life. The despicable dog poisoner is always among us, and it is difficult to know where and when he will strike next.

One variation of food refusal includes teaching your dog to eat food that is given in a specific dish. He would be taught to refuse food offered in a dish made of different material, such as porcelain vs. stainless steel. Another method teaches the dog to take food only from the left hand. Of course, if the dog poisoner is one of the five per cent of the population that is left-handed, this will not help.

For optimum safety and peace of mind, when teaching food refusal or poison proofing, teach your dog to ignore food that is found on the ground. Most food poisoning occurs when doctored meat is tossed over the back yard fence.

When protection or security dogs are taught food refusal, they learn to snap at any person who tries to tempt their palates. This technique, while excellent for high security work, is completely out of place for a household pet. Security dogs work in areas with all kinds of physical controls to keep them away from foolish but well-meaning people. Anyone who gets close enough to offer food to a security dog is up to no good. Thus poison proofing can save a guard dog's life, while stopping a thief. In many of these situations the dog is patrolling an area without a handler. To prepare him for this work, he has been agitated and continues to be agitated every time a stranger presents him with food.

Your dog should turn away, not snap, when food is presented. A dog that is well grounded in obedience work will learn this exercise very rapidly. Start off with the dog on leash, wearing a metal collar. Have him approached, in a friendly manner, by one of your co-conspirators, who will be holding some meat in his hand. Your friend has been briefed and understands that Spartan must not get the piece of roast beef, no matter what. The chunk of meat is offered, and when your dog reaches for it, give a sharp jerk on his collar and say NO! Spartan will be approached three or four times, and then the young man will go away. Sit down, smoke a cigarette, relax, and then let your assistant return with the same piece of beef. Ideally, you should use a different "troublemaker" each time if possible. But most people find that using the same person is a necessity, particularly if the dog is mean-looking.

Another session follows with your assistant attempting to give food to Spartan. Occasionally, he will give Spartan a slap on the muzzle as the dog reaches for the food. This quick slap will replace your leash correction as the training progresses. By doing the training in this manner most of the corrections will be leash corrections. There are a number of reasons why this is preferable to having most of the corrections come from the poison proofer.

1. You know your dog best and should be able to time your corrections much better than your assistant could unless he is a professional trainer.
2. It is preferable whenever possible to discipline your own dog yourself.
3. There is less chance for an inexperienced person to injure your dog if his corrections are kept to a minimum.

4. There is less chance for an inexperienced person to get injured if your dog is highly protective over his food.

It is necessary, however, to have the assistant do some of the corrections for poison proofing to work. Spartan must realize that you do not have to be there when he is corrected for thinking about sinking his canines into a piece of rare steak.

Now, even though it is your first session, you can start on the next phase of the training. This is really an easy trick. Sit down, take a break, and light another cigarette. If you don't smoke, it is not necessary to start to accomplish this trick. In fact, if you do, getting yourself to quit is an even better trick. But that's another book! For now, have your assistant repeat the routine with the meat. Spartan is no dummy and will probably turn his head away. *Voilà!* The trick is taught. No! You have a long way to go. Now have your assistant throw the meat on the ground. Hold the leash so that it is loose, and let Spartan feel that he can get to the food. In reality, he will not have enough rope to hang himself. Furthermore, you will be on guard and ready to correct him with a NO and a sharp jerk if he gives in to temptation. Should he succeed in getting the meat, pounce on him, force his jaws open, and extract the meat. If you are afraid that you will not be able to do this, don't bother to begin poison proofing your dog. Getting the food out of Spartan's mouth is the name of the game. If he is able to swallow an occasional piece of meat, that will give him enough incentive to take chances—and the value of this work will be destroyed. This is hard work, but that's why we gave you all those breaks. After you've jumped in and removed the meat from your dog's mouth, give him a series of jerks on the leash accompanied by a severe tongue-lashing. We are dealing with poisoned meat and this is no joke! As far as your dog is concerned, this is the real thing. A word of caution: your dog should have been taught to give up his food to you. If you have not done this first, do it before you begin this training. Do not pounce on a dog who is very protective over his food.

If Spartan ignores the meat, try walking him over it a few times. Do not Heel him over it, since he already knows that he must ignore things on the ground when heeling. Keep him on a loose leash so that he has the opportunity and the temptation to sniff at the meat or grab for it. At this point you can give him enough length of leash so that he can be sneaky. But you will be alert and prepared. If he slips, you know what to do.

The first session is now over—and well done, too. Now what can you do with this beat-up piece of roast beef? As dog trainer and owner, you can feed it to Spartan, in your left hand or in his own dish, whichever is your training goal.

When Spartan is presented with the hunk of meat properly, tell him OKAY and praise him when he takes it. So far, so good. Alas, you are not finished yet. Your work has only begun. Although you may be impressed with your progress in such a short period of time, this is a trick that must be worked on continually.

In your next session, try to have a different assistant. He will start off the same way that your first assistant did. Finally, throw the meat on the ground. Spartan knows what is expected and he will ignore the meat.

These sessions have been rather short, but now you will have to spend more time working on food refusal. Find a good hiding place from which you can observe Spartan in the back yard. This hiding place will have to be close enough and with good direct access so that you can explode onto the scene and correct any of Spartan's transgressions. The first time you try this, have one of your able assistants tempt the dog. Spartan, in all likelihood, will refuse the food. Next, have your assistant toss the meat into the back yard. Watch Spartan! He may give the meat some side glances or he may ignore it. Should he go for the meat at any time, charge into the back yard, shouting NO, NO, NO, NO, NO. Grab him, force open his mouth, plunge your hand inside, scoop out the meat, and give him a resounding shaking, again repeating NO, NO, NO! Now you can sit down and relax, but don't be too swift to make up with your dog. This phase of the training is tough, but if you are ready to throw in the towel, remember that this is not just one more trick. It really may save your dog's life one day. Besides, this is much harder on you than it is on Spartan. He lounges in his yard while you sneak around spying on him. If he does something that is quite natural, you have to act unnatural. You have to spring into action, expend all kind of energy, and then work hard getting your blood pressure back to normal! Nevertheless, training *must* be maintained. Once this trick is learned, it will be easy to keep your dog sharp—and it is more important to do so than to work on any other phase of training with him. Tests should be run at least once a month under realistic conditions. Only then can you rest assured that your beloved pet is really safe from the occasional lunatic who would poison an innocent and unsuspecting animal.

16. Tricks with Class

You know that your dog has good breeding. Whether his line goes back to American and Canadian Champion Cummings' Gold-Rush Charlie or straight to the Brooklyn ASPCA, he's tops in your eyes. But these tricks are just as apt to show off *your* class as his. They are witty, intelligent, and all have a very special flair. Why do them in your living room when you could do them at Bloomingdale's or the Top of the Mark?

CALCULUS

Rush out and buy a pocket calculator. If you're anything like us, you'll never get through this trick without one. This trick is an advanced variation of SPEAK, COUNT, ADD (in Chapter 11). Your cues will be the same but your material will be a lot jazzier. Why ask your dog to add one and two, when for the same effort on his part you can ask him the square root of nine? Do you follow our drift? With a little help from Texas Instruments, you can make your dog look like a genius. He probably is one anyway.

On the other hand, if you want to skip the calculator, you can figure out a few toughies in advance of your performance and have them up your sleeve. Unless you're a mathematical wizard, don't ask for questions from the audience. You can play around with square roots. Or you can fool around with magic numbers, like so:

Nine is a magic number. Watch how it works. A friend comes to visit and has heard about Einstein, your trick dog. Bring Einstein into the room and tell your friend, "You are going on a shopping trip. You can take as much money with you as you like—as long as it's over a dollar and less than ten dollars. So don't go to Tiffany's. Write down the number but don't let me see it—and don't let Einstein see it. Now reverse the number. ($7.69 becomes $9.67) Einstein is generous. He says you can have the higher figure

($9.67) as spending money. The lower figure ($7.69) is what you'll actually spend. So deduct the lower from the higher to see what you'll have left over. ($1.98) Now tell the dollar figure to Einstein ($1) and he'll tell you the change." Here comes the magic. Your middle number will always be nine. The first and last numbers will always add up to nine. Turn to Einstein and have him bark nine times. Now deduct the dollar figure from nine to get the last number. (8) Have Einstein bark that number. Now go on, after your bow and applause, to something else. Repeating tricks is dangerous, particularly magic tricks.

If you're hooked on this kind of fun with numbers, rush out this time and buy Royal Heath's *Mathemagic: Magic, Puzzles and Games with Numbers* and Martin Gardner's *Mathematics, Magic and Mystery,* both published by Dover Publications, New York. These two should teach you and Einstein everything you've always wanted to know about wowing your friends with number tricks. So next time your dog has nothing to do, give him one of these to chomp on. They're chock full of food for thought.

FOREIGN LANGUAGE TRICKS

You don't need a crash course at Berlitz to do this classy trick with your dog. You'll get it right here.

Remember how you taught your dog to spell? The same principles work

ENGLISH	GERMAN	DUTCH	SWEDISH	RUSSIAN	POLISH
Beg or sit high	"Mach Schoen" (Mack Scherm)	"Bedel" (Bay' del)	"Tigga" (Tee gah')	"Сять Красиьо" (Sat Krace'-vah)	"Poproś" (Póprush)
Speak	"Wie spricht der Hund?" (Vee sprickt der Hoont)	"Spreek" (Sprayk)	"Skäll" (Shell)	"Голос" (Goll'-us)	"Daj Głos" (Dai gwós)
Roll over	"Dreh dich" (Dray dish)	"Rol om" (Roll um)	"Rulla över" (Rooh-lah-oev-ah')	"Перевернись" (Perry ver-neeś)	"Przewrót" (Pschévrot)
Fetch	"Bring" (Brring)	"Breng 't" (Brang et)	"Bring" (Brring)	"Аппорт" (Ap-port)	"Aport" (Áport)
Give your paw	"Gib Fuss" (Gib foos)	"Pootje" (Po'-cha)	"Vacker Tass" (Vack-ah tasś)	"Дае Лапу" (Dye Lapoo)	"Daj łape" (Dai wapeh)
Play dead	"Sei tot" (Sigh toat)	"Dood" (Doadt)	"Spela Död" (Speel-ah' doit)	"Замри" (Zam Rhee)	"Połóż się" (Powoosh z sheh)
Say your prayers	"Bete" (Bay-tah)	"Zeg je gebed" (Seck ya gä-bet)	"Sitt vackert" (Sit vah-kert)	"Помолиси" (Po-mah-leeś)	"Spiewaj" (Shpi-e-vei)
Hup (to jump)	"Hopp" (Hopp)	"Spring" (Sprring)	"Hoppa" (Hopp-ah')	"Барьер" (Barr-yehŕ)	"Przeszkoda" (Pshesh koda)
Crawl	"Kriechen" (Kree-chen)	"Kruip" (Krype)	"Kråla" (Krawl-ah')	"Полэи" (Pal-zeh)	"Czołgaj się" (Chógai sheh)

The foreign language spellings of the commands are in quotation marks. Immediately below, in parentheses, are the phonetic spellings of the words. These are not literal translations but the actual commands that trainers in these countries use. For example, the command to beg in German is literally translated as "Make pretty." The German command for speak is "How speaks the dog?" as shown above.

For those of you who are wondering about the lack of Romance languages, it is interesting to note that these languages, while excellent for making love, are too soft to give a good command in. Before this book is banned in the French Canadian Provinces, note that the French Army gives their dogs German commands and people in Central and South America generally train their dogs to respond to English or German commands.

in this trick. Either train little Bourek directly in another language or train him first in English, teach him hand signals, and hand signal to him as you teach him his commands in Polish. Soon enough you will be able to tell him *siad* (shaht) and he'll sit. Remember, as with your own knowledge of another language, if you don't use it, *he'll* lose it. So enjoy, enjoy. To the left is your introductory linguistics course, on the house.

CRAWL

Crawl is taught to military dogs and scout dogs. It is particularly important when a dog and his soldier handler have to crawl under enemy fire with an urgent message. We hope that you are not going to run into that type of problem. But if you are ever "under fire" and want to take the heat off, crawl makes a very cute trick.

Begin with your dog in the Down position and then lie down alongside him. Place your left hand on the leash, about at the spot where the snap joins the collar. It is especially important for this exercise that your dog Rip is well grounded in his obedience training. If he is not doing a reliable Down, stay away from this trick until he is. A dog's propensity to nip is greater in this exercise than in many others. So proceed with caution. Grasp the leash and collar firmly between the palm and the thumb. Give the command CRAWL and move your hand forward while it remains parallel to the ground. Rip will start to get up and you must pull down on the collar rapidly while repeating CRAWL and then making a forward "come on" motion with your left hand. When you do this, your dog will crawl for a very short distance. Heap praise upon him!

At the first lesson, happily accept a three-inch crawl. As the training progresses, the length that you will require Rip to crawl will increase. The problem that you will have to fight patiently and consistently is that he will continually pop up. That is okay and to be expected. As soon as he jumps up, force him down again. Repeat the moving hand signal, "come on," and the verbal command CRAWL. So far, you are still crawling with Rip. Once he can crawl a few feet with you at his side, you can put him on a Down Stay and walk six inches in front of him. Keep his leash on him and hold your hand over the leash so that you are exerting some downward pressure. Tell Rip CRAWL. He should now crawl right up to you for praise. Praise him willingly and warmly. Continue to extend the distance that your dog will crawl to you. Eventually you can have him crawl fifteen or twenty feet off leash. If ever he begins to pop up, move in quickly and jerk downward on the leash, repeating the command firmly. If he starts to rebel when off leash, continue the on-leash work for a while longer.

This trick can be integrated with a couple of others for a dazzling routine. Your company or audience is watching as Rip performs another trick. Suddenly, you pull your finger from your "holster," point it at him, and say BANG! On the first BANG, he lifts one paw and begins to LIMP. On the second BANG, Rip drops to the ground and crawls. The third "shot" is the coup de grâce—Rip rolls over and plays dead. Now you know why his name is R.I.P.

LIMP

This classy trick looks terrific by itself, but when combined with a variety of other tricks, it gives the look of a professional routine. Don't pass it by. Besides, you never know when your "limping dog" will give you just the edge you need in a touchy situation.

Louise has her collar and leash on. As you stand in front of her and facing her, loop the leash under one of her forelegs so that you can elevate her leg at the wrist. Gently pull up on the leash so that she must raise her foreleg. Her wrist, supported by the leash, should be held slightly above her elbow. Now call her to come to you. LOUISE, COME. GOOD GIRL. LIMP. If she takes a few steps toward you on three legs, praise her, let her rest, and try again. As you practice the limp and as Louise catches on, begin

Get your dog's attention.

Point your finger and say LIMP. *Rippy Grznar—English Setter*

to try her off leash. Make a sling with the leash and support her wrist as you call her to come to you and limp. Your work will be accomplished and you can begin to use the trick when Louise will limp off leash, no strings attached.

Is it worth spending time on this trick? You never can tell. Someday your poor, limping dog may get you out of a speeding ticket. In the meantime, don't drive too fast and try these winning combinations:

1. The Classic—LIMP, CRAWL, PLAY DEAD (see Crawl, above, for details). To facilitate this combination, teach the dog a hand signal for Limp that resembles a "gun." Point at your dog for Limp and "shoot" her, point again, shoot again, and she Crawls. Point again—BANG— *voilà!* DEAD DOG.
2. Escape Clause—When doing math or magic tricks, if one doesn't work out, signal Louise to LIMP and beat it!
3. Loaded Dice—Send your limping dog to help you pick up that someone special passing in the street (see Report, in Chapter 17).
4. Geriatric Comedy Special—Signal your old dog to limp, send her for her Geritol, and then have her do a few jumping tricks. Write the company that makes Geritol and tell them. You may get a free case of their product.
5. Pass the Hat—Have your trick dog serve snacks in a basket and then limp around collecting tips. Who could turn down a limping dog?
6. The Power of Prayer—Your dog is limping. Tell her SAY YOUR PRAYERS and then have her run around on all fours. That's class!

More? Your turn.

CARRY A BUCKET OF CHAMPAGNE

This elegant trick is one that elegant dogs cannot do. This trick requires the services of a huge, macho type of dog such as the Bull Mastiff, Newfoundland, or St. Bernard. The Saint is highly recommended because of his long history of bringing alcoholic beverages to stranded travelers.

Remember that this is a trick with class. Don't practice your dog with beer bottles, full or empty. The neighbors might see what you were doing and your image would be forever ruined. Atlas is going to learn to carry a full liter of champagne, chilled and corked, in a heavy metal ice bucket. In order to accomplish this, he will have to be much more than a reliable retriever. He will have to be the Charles Atlas of the dog world. If he's the skinny little runt who gets sand kicked in his face, don't bust his chops with this difficult work.

This will not be the only trick you teach Atlas. In order for him to suc-

cessfully carry a bucket of champagne, he will have had to whet his whistle on lighter items first. He will need a strong desire to please you, a good working relationship with you, and, possibly, a sense of the ridiculous. If this trick doesn't knock out your guests, think about revising your guest list before the next champagne dinner.

Atlas will have to be a big bruiser for another reason, too. He must be able to make the bucket clear the ground. A powerful Basset might be able to hold the weight of the bucket and bottle, but he would wind up dragging the bucket along the ground—a not very classy trick.

Ready to begin? If your brute is still a puppy, you can start him off with the removable handle of a bucket. In this way, he will get used to carrying the handle around before you add the weight. The handle is strong and sturdy. You can hang any number of things from it to get Atlas used to toting. Finally, put it back onto the bucket and have Atlas carry that. He is, of course, a retriever and you have these skills under your belt as well. Once you have him carrying the empty bucket, begin to add some weight to it. You can begin with some ice cubes—he has to get used to the noise, too. Now it's time to introduce an empty champagne bottle. If you don't have enough class to have champagne empties lying around, why bother with this trick?

Now Atlas can carry the bucket with an empty champagne bottle in it. Gradually add ice, thus adding to the weight he can carry. Now it's time to introduce a full bottle of champagne, imported if your prefer. If Atlas shrugs off this extra weight, he qualifies as a truly classy dog. Quick—to the phone. You don't want to waste all his talent and you don't want to drink all that chilled champagne by yourself! Seat your company and summon Atlas with the champagne. If he has real class, he'll run back into the kitchen and emerge with a pressed dish towel to wrap the bottle in. Don't expect him to show up with a corkscrew. This dog has experience and he knows how champagne bottles open.

17. Tricks with Sass

Technically, *sass* means talking back or talking disrespectfully. Would we ever tell you or your dog to do that? Certainly not. To us, there's nothing quite so refreshing as a sassy kid—especially if he's not ours. Sass can mean humor mixed with cheekiness. It can mean just enough impudence to be charming—especially when executed by a dog. Would we ever tell you or your dog to do that? You bet!

EAT AT THE TABLE

Most dog-training books will tell you, "Don't feed your dog at the table!" You probably heard it from your mother long before you ever read a dog-training book. So we're going to tell you how to get your dog to eat at the table—with both sass and class. After all, no one wants to dine with a dog who has poor table manners!

You don't *have* to teach your dog to eat at the table. Some fastidious people wouldn't dream of it. But if you favor impractical jokes or if you live alone, this might just be your cup of tea. If you can't think of more than three reasons *not* to have a dog as a dining companion, proceed as follows. First and foremost, Emily Post, your American Mixed Breed, must learn to sit on a chair. You'll need a chair that is very steady to make Emily feel safe and secure. But don't let her jump up onto the chair whenever she wants to —only on command. Occasionally, you might have a dinner guest who would prefer not to sit at the table discussing the President's economic policies with a dog. If you let Emily hop onto the chair at will, she may just decide to proceed to the tabletop and lie down next to the turkey. Tell her GET IN YOUR CHAIR as you pull the chair out for her. When she is sitting pretty and feeling steady, say STAY and slowly push the chair closer to the table. Move the chair slowly and repeat STAAAY, as the unsteadiness of the moving chair may make her a bit nervous. Now, do you think Emily should sit with her forelegs on the table? We think all four legs should be on the chair! There's nothing quite so uncouth as a dog who puts her paws on the tablecloth. However, if your Emily is a tiny toy, we'll make an exception. It's better than having her sit on a phone book!

A large cloth napkin should be worn about Emily's neck, tucked securely into her collar. Most trained dogs won't object, but give her a few minutes to get used to it. If her paws are up on the table and that's a no-no, tell her just that. Of course, Emily will not start until you give her the word—and the word in this case is OKAY. But what are you two going to eat? It's rude to serve separate meals to guests—and since we don't care for dog cuisine, try the following recipe to delight both your palate and hers:

DOG FOOD RECIPE*

1 onion
1 pound ground beef
2 ribs celery
Water chestnuts
Garlic
Soy sauce
1 cup brown rice
Chinese noodles

Braise onion and then chopped beef in a frying pan. Add chopped celery and sliced water chestnuts. Season to taste with garlic and soy sauce. Cook rice and add to meat mixture. Place in Dutch oven and heat over a low flame for 10 minutes. Serve over Chinese noodles for added crunch. Eat with chopsticks (or without).

* Serves: One adult human and one Brittany Spaniel
or
One adult human and two Cairn Terriers
or
Two adult humans and one Chihuahua
or
One Rhodesian Ridgeback
or
One child and two Dachshunds (smooth, wire, or long-haired)
or
Two children and one Shih Tzu

Emily will need a deeper dish than you will to help prevent spills. If she gobbles too fast, tell her "EEEASY, SLOW," and if you must, take her food away for a moment. Now you're doing fine. Emily appreciates your cooking, perhaps a bit more than most of your other guests. Now you never need eat alone again—and you can charm small guests at your next children's birthday party. But unless you're sassier than we are, better keep Emily on the floor when Mom comes for dinner!

An occasional guest may prefer not to discuss politics with a dog.

TUG IT

This versatile trick can also be a game and exercise for your dog. Many pet shops carry a figure-eight rubber dog toy that is a favorite with many dogs. Breeds such as the Boxer and Bull Terrier go wild over this game. A tug-of-war starts between you and your dog. Some dogs even enjoy being lifted off the ground and spun around!

Extend the figure eight toward Sheba and tell her TUG IT. Once she grabs hold of the toy, a gentle pressure is applied. The harder your dog pulls, the harder you pull. After your dog is used to the command and the figure eight, you can switch to other materials. A burlap sack, once a standby at feed stores, is an excellent tool for tugging exercise. However, they are hard to find, as they are rapidly being replaced by plastic bags. If you cannot hunt down some burlap, try a clothesline. Make a circle out of the rope or, if you are handy with rope, duplicate the figure eight. Offer Sheba the rope, saying TUG IT. To keep the game interesting, try the sack or an old piece of towel. Let Sheba tug on the material and then pull it from your hands. Most dogs will shake their prize—and you can take advantage of this, saying SHAKE IT. However, control is important. You do not want Sheba grabbing at everything that goes past her. Be sure to practice getting her to let go on command. See the Out section in Fetch on Command (in Chapter 2).

So far, this exercise has been more like a game than a trick. Now you can tie a short piece of rope to a cardboard box or small wagon and tell Sheba TUG IT. Gradually add some weight to the box and encourage Sheba to TUG IT. In the winter, Sheba can do her trick outdoors and pull a sled for your children. She can even bring home a wagon full of groceries, with you walking at her side, hands free. With a little extra work, she will tug another dog's leash and help you obedience train your next dog. Or, if you've taught her to read, leave this book lying around and see if she decides to teach your new dog more tricks than you taught her!

Most dogs love this game. *Puppy Cordes—German Shepherd*

REPORT

This is a trick that is all at once practical, silly, and deeply romantic. It's purpose is to enable both men and women to meet one another in a quick and respectable fashion. In truth, it works best for very beautiful women and extremely handsome men, but it can also work for people like us. The best ingredient is a puppy, but any cute dog will do.

You'll need some co-conspirators to help you teach this trick to Cupid. Your friend should have some dog treats in his hand. Take your puppy about five feet away from your friend and face him toward your friend. Give him a start in the right direction and say REPORT. If necessary, your friend can even call Cupid, but this crutch should be eliminated early in the training. When Cupid reaches your friend, your friend should reward Cupid with treats, pet him, praise him, and fuss over him. Gradually increase the distance until you are twenty-five feet or more away from your friend. Facing the dog in the right direction is extremely important, as you don't want to point and be obvious when you see a potential heartthrob walking down the street. Are you getting the picture? Fine.

Continue to practice. Cupid reports to different friends and each time gets praised for doing so. Remember that young puppies will learn this trick rather quickly, but if the distance is great, they may begin on their journey and then forget where they are going. Even though puppies are especially appealing, you are probably better off with a cute older dog—especially if you want to use this trick for a steady stream of dates. Some cute puppies grow up rapidly into formidable-looking adults.

Now the choice is yours. Stroll down the avenue with Cupid and keep your eye out for Robert Redford or Farrah. Tell Cupid to REPORT, and as he wiggles up to the person of your choice, go quickly to retrieve him. "I'm terribly sorry! Thanks a million for catching my dog. I don't know what I'd do without him—I'm all alone in this strange town and he's such great company . . ." Sorry. More than this we cannot do for you. You'll have to work out your own follow-up line. And Good Luck!

SNEEZE

The old standby "Wait until your dog does it and then give him the command" is ineffective here. Just how often does your dog sneeze? Induce your dog to sneeze and then say AHHHH SNEEZE. The AHHHH portion of the command makes it look like *you* are going to sneeze and does more than get you in the mood. It makes the trick more dramatic and interesting. You can toss your head back and then forward, sneezing out the command. You and Sneezy can do sneezing duets.

There are two basic approaches to induce your dog to sneeze on command, with variations on both. First, you can give your dog something that will make him sneeze. Pepper is excellent. Use it sparingly and not too frequently. Put a small quantity in your cupped hand. If your palm is a little sweaty, that's okay. It will keep the pepper on your hand and you will have less falling on the floor. Cup your hand over your dog's nose and say AHHHH SNEEZE. Keep your hand there until Sneezy obliges, and then rapidly pull it away and praise him profusely. Do this no more than twice in succession. After a short while, you'll find that a cupped hand without pepper in it will get your dog to sneeze, too.

But pepper tends to be messy and may even get *you* to sneeze. Try the second method first. Put your hand around your dog's muzzle and blow into his nostrils. This will get most dogs to sneeze and is easier on the dog and the kitchen floor. Of course, don't try this with a biting dog. (Shame on you if your Sneezy is a biter. Why are you fooling around with tricks?) A variation that works with many dogs is simply to blow in the dog's face, anywhere around the nose. Different dogs sneeze at different spots, so experiment and blast away. What can you do with this trick? Remember, we call it a Trick with Sass. Think cheeky and punch it up with a sassy patter.

"NOTHING" TRICK

The "nothing" trick is a perfect ending for all your hard work. If you've gotten this far (without skipping around), you're one heck of a dog trainer. So here's some frosting for your cake!

This trick looks swell on a soulful-looking dog. It's also great on slow-moving dogs like Saints, Newfs, Great Pyreneeses, and Mastiffs. Play up your dog's looks to make the trick better. If your dog is slow, ask him to do things that take great energy and agility. If he's a Chihuahua, tell him KILL! Never fear—he won't. Read on.

Command your trick dog BOZO, FETCH, tossing your wallet. Bozo looks at you and does nothing. BOZO, you say falteringly, SIT UP AND BEG. Bozo rolls over and plays dead. BOZO, HOW OLD IS MY MOTHER-IN-LAW? Perhaps Bozo yawns. Get out the hoop. Tell your audience, "You've got to see this one. This is his best trick. He did this one on the Johnny Carson Show. BOZO, JUMP THROUGH THE HOOP." Bozo stays in the dead dog position.

How, you ask, is this master trick achieved? How many months will I have to work with my dog to wow my friends with this one? Simple? Yes and no. First of all, all the commands are wrong. (Did we fool you, too?) Your dog has learned to retrieve on the words TAKE IT, sit up and beg on the command SIT HIGH, jump a hoop on the command OVER. (Can you take it from here?) Second, your dog's name is Fred, not Bozo. Third, you are giving him not only incorrect verbal commands, but contrary hand signals. Either place Fred on a Sit Stay, or hand signal him to play dead, and then it's all in the patter. The trick can be as funny as *you* can be. BOZO, you can plead, BRING US SOME BEER. BOZO, DISAPPEAR!

This is *your* act. Fred is the window dressing that will make your wit explode into greatness. Have fun—the sky's the limit on this one.

18. Tricks for the Twenty-first Century

Times have changed and so our friend the dog, willing and adaptable, has changed too. Hardly a hound nowadays gets to run before the horses in hot pursuit of a fox. Schipperkes now get excited when they see their leash instead of when they smell the sea. And what self-respecting modern Poodle gets to retrieve from water for a living? He'd risk getting rejected by his groomer! Modern dogs relate to modern things. They wake up when the alarm clock rings. They rush to the front door when the answering machine gets turned on. Many get vacuumed instead of brushed. Nowadays, dog and machine have to live in harmony—or at least try. These two modern tricks put dog and machine together for some sci-fi type of wacky humor. Try them on for size.

THE ANSWERING MACHINE TRICK

In the "old days" it was "his master's voice" that turned on the little Fox Terrier, now an advertising classic. Now it's your canine's voice that will turn on your friends or clients. While answering machines are growing rapidly in popularity, many people are still upset at the thought of talking to a recording. They freeze up and they hang up.

Now you and Spock can relax your callers with a laugh and get far more messages and fewer hang-ups. Begin your announcement recording with Spock, your star trick dog of the future. Press your Record button and signal Spock to speak. After a few well-placed barks, record your message. Then signal Spock again and let him bark goodbye. It's more than a good goof. People will enjoy barking back to your unique machine. Why trek all over town for a solution. Your fate is in your dog, not in your stars!

CB TRICK

If you want your canine good buddy in on the CB craze, first give him a good handle. It would show a complete lack of class to have him on the air as plain old Fido. Whether you decide to call him the Bionic Basenji, the Whispering Whippet, or the Westminster Water Spaniel, his good name will be half the fun.

Of course, your Talking Tervuren speaks on command! So now he can lay some good numbers on all your good buddies. But don't turn him into a ratchet jaw. Be brief, play it cool, and have some fun.

Next time you're asked your handle, give yours *and* your seat cover's. Your Talking Tervuren can bark back a 10-36, with minimum help from you. He can "say" where you pull the plug. And he can sign off with a loud and clear 10-4. Perhaps you'll even arrange to meet the Terrible Terrier at your next pit stop. Why not goof a little with your dog and your CB? But don't be a Harvey Wallbanger and don't collect Green Stamps. 10-4 good buddy.

Ratchet jaw	Someone who never stops talking
Handle	Name
Seat cover	Passenger
10-36	Correct time
Pull the plug	Your exit
Pit stop	Gas station
Harvy Wallbanger	Wreckless driver
Green stamps	Tickets

Any dog can be a good buddy.

19. Dirty Tricks

No book on tricks written during this age of political surprises would be complete without a section such as this. The winning combination is this: a dog's natural and beautiful innocence added to the low trickery, deceit, and sneakiness that are too often a part of human nature as we find it in our times. We can't resist this obvious but delicious opportunity and we're betting that you can't either. So if you enjoy dirty tricks, please limit yourself to these.

A DIRTY TRICK FOR INTELLECTUALS

If you play chess and you like to horse around, this baby is for you. Set up the trick in the following way: your dog will always work the side of the board opposite from where you are sitting. His signal will be your cough— but do it up right. Since this is truly a dirty trick, the dog must appear to be doing this trick without you watching or signaling him. Furthermore, if your opponent sees the dog working, you have a funny trick. If he doesn't see the dog, you have a low-down dirty trick. So when you cough into your over-sized handkerchief, make it an oversized cough. Face away from the board —it's rude to cough in someone's face even if it is a fake cough—and make your coughing fit so dramatic that your opponent looks at you, not at Satan. On this cue, Satan will trot over to the chessboard and "pinch" your opponent's rook. When Satan has the rook, recover from your fit and win the game. Do not under any circumstances let your opponent fetch you a glass of water. If he leaves the room and returns to find a missing rook, you have not a dirty trick but a tacky situation to get out of.

Now let's teach Satan to steal that rook. The rook is a good piece to work with because it is a valuable piece and sits, at least for a while, in an accessible spot. To make things easier for Satan, and to make sure he never swipes *your* rook, teach him to work the far right corner of the board. That will mean that he is to pick up the king's rook if your opponent plays black and the queen's rook if he has white.

Satan must be a willing and reliable retriever if you want to start winning at chess the easy way. Begin with an empty board and place a rook at the far right square. Tell Satan TAKE IT and praise him. Try him on this simple routine a few times a day for a few days. Once he is lifting the chess piece with the stealthiness and pride of a cat burglar, go into your coughing routine to make him do it. Give the command and cough. Gradually drop the command. Praise profusely. But now what is Satan to do with his stolen treasure? Surely, you don't want him to chew it up. You might be playing black next game. Do you have an umbrella stand? A large ashtray? A wastebasket close by? Find a receptacle and have him deposit his trophy there. This will take a bit of work, but it is an important part of the trick—especially if others are watching. Cough. Satan will take the rook. Lead him to the umbrella stand. Tell him OUT and let the rook fall—ping—into the stand. Praise. Play with Satan. Try it again.

As you work, teach Satan only one step at a time. Try not to rush him or get him confused. Once he's an accomplished thief, the cough should send him automatically from beginning to end. What a classy way to get odds!

When you try this out on company, be sure to exaggerate your cough into a large handkerchief to start the ball rolling. Your friends will marvel at your dog's compassion and helpfulness. Your dog will enjoy doing a new routine. Your opponent will never play chess with you again—unless he's a bit inattentive. In that case, at long last, you'll be winning at chess!

PUT OUT A MATCH OR NO SMOKING ALLOWED

Nonsmokers may argue that this is not a dirty trick. They will testify that preventing someone from smoking is a great favor to that person and all those around. Nevertheless, for all you smokers, we are calling this a dirty trick.

This is a trick that some dogs teach themselves because of their strong dislike for fire and smoke. With a little work and the right dog, this can be an impressive and unique trick. While this trick might look best on a Dalmatian, the traditional Firehouse Dog, it is best done with any dog that has a stronger-than-ordinary hatred of smoke and fire.

Begin with Danny on a leash and a box of wooden matches handy. You will need to have control of Danny as you strike the match. Strike it against the side of the box with your right hand while holding the leash in your left. Draw Danny in toward the match. Now watch his reactions. If he shows any dislike of the fire, praise. If he barks or sneezes, shake out the flame and praise him warmly. Any action such as a bark or a sneeze that will drive air

Dirty trick or favor? *Freckles Zaretsky—Dalmatian Mix*

toward the match can put out the flame and should therefore be praised. The trick is to extinguish the fire. It does not matter *how* it is done—only *that* it is done. If your dog hates fire or loves you enough to put out a match, let him do it in whatever style he chooses.

What if there is no reaction to the lit match? Give it a shake and, while it is still smoking, hold it under Danny's nostrils. This should produce a reaction rather quickly. If Danny paws at the smoking match, praise him and pull it away immediately. There is double rewarding with this trick. As usual, you will praise the dog for doing what you want him to do. In addition, you will remove the hated match. From Danny's point of view, the second reward will be more rewarding than the first!

If Danny paws at the match now when you light it, just let him hit it once. While the pads of his feet are leatherlike, the hair between them can get singed. However, one quick brush against a match will not hurt your dog. This action can be compared to putting out a candle between your wet thumb and forefinger or passing a finger through a flame. Still, be careful and don't overdo. If your dog hits your hand and not the match, that can put out the flame too. Any slight wind or motion that puts out the match is praiseworthy and will earn Danny some fine petting and the removal of the smell he so dislikes.

Once Danny can proficiently put out a match, you can set him to work on your friends who smoke. Let him know he can put out any match he sees. Why not? Encourage him. It might come in very handy one day if your kids like to play with fire! Now when guests plop on your couch and get ready to pollute the atmosphere in your living room, Danny can go to work. What a clever way to say that you mind very much when they smoke!

TRICK APTITUDE CHART

This chart is not meant as a judgment on the worth of dog breeds, but as a guide for the novice to help him to select the easiest tricks for his dog. The fact that a dog rates a high aptitude on certain tricks should not be the basis for determining if you want this breed for a house pet. Furthermore, if the dog has a low aptitude for a trick and you have high determination, you can still teach the trick.

Most dogs can do any trick not listed here. For aptitude in carrying and bringing tricks, see Retrieving Tricks (Chapter 2). The code for the chart is as follows:

> h—high aptitude
> a—average
> l—low
> f—forget it!

Trick Aptitude Chart

The Sporting Breeds	Retrieving	Water retrieving	Scent discrimination	Beg	Play dead	Walk on hindq.	Sing	Push a carriage	Speaking tricks	Agility tricks	Circus tricks	Jump rope	Bark at intruders	Crawl	Jumping
Griffon, Wirehaired Pointing	h	h	h	a	a	a	h	a	a	h	a	a	a	a	h
Pointer	a+	a	h	a	a	a	a	a	a	h	a	a	a	a	h
Pointer, German Short Haired	h	h	h	a	a	a	h	a	h	h	a	h	h	h	h
Pointer, German Wirehaired	h	h	h	a	a	a	h	a	a	h	a	a	a	h	h
Retriever, Chesapeake Bay	h	h+	h	a	l	a	a	a	h	h	h	a	h+	l	a
Retriever, Curly Coated	h+	h+	h	a	a	a	a	a	a	h	a	a	a	a	a
Retriever, Flat Coated	h+	h+	h	h	a	h	a	h	h	h	a	l	a	a	h
Retriever, Golden	h+	h+	h	h	h	a	a	l	h	h	a	l	a+	a	h
Retriever, Labrador	h+	h+	h	a	a—	a	a	l	h	h	a	l	a+	a	h
Setter, English	h	a+	h	a	a	a	a	a	a	h	a	a	a	a—	h
Setter, Gordon	h—	a	h	a	a	a	a	a	a	a	a	a	a	a	a
Setter, Irish	a	a	h	h	l	a	a	a	h	h	a	a	a	a	h
Spaniel, American Water	h	h	h	a	a+	a	a	a	a	a	a	a	a	h	a
Spaniel, Brittany	h	h	h	h	l	a	a	a	h	a	h	h	a	a	a+
Spaniel, Clumber	h	a	h	a	h+	l	a	l	l	f	f	f	l	a	l
Spaniel, Cocker	h	a	h	h	a	h	h	h	h	a	a	l	a	h	a
Spaniel, English Cocker	h	a	h	h	a	a	a	a	a	a+	a	a	a	h	h—
Spaniel, English Springer	h	h	h	h	l	a	a	a	a	h	a	h	h	h	h
Spaniel, Field	h	a	h	a+	h	a	a	a	a	l	l	l	a	h	l
Spaniel, Irish Water	h	h+	h	h	h	h	h	h	h	h	h	h	h—	h	h
Spaniel, Sussex	h	a	h	a	h	a	l	a	a	a	a	a	a	a	a
Spaniel, Welsh Springer	a	a	a	h	h	a	a	a	h	a	h	a	a	h	h
Vizsla	h	h	h	a	a	a	h	a	h	h—	a	l	l	h	h
Weimaraner	h	h	h	h	a	h—	h	h	h	h	h	h	a+	a—	h

The Hound Breeds	Retrieving	Water retrieving	Scent discrimination	Beg	Play dead	Walk on hindq.	Sing	Push a carriage	Speaking tricks	Agility tricks	Circus tricks	Jump rope	Bark at intruders	Crawl	Jumping
Afghan Hound	a	l	l	l	h	l	l	l	l	h	a	l	l	h	h
Basenji	l	l	l	h	a	h	h	a	f	a	l	f	f	a	a
Basset Hound	a	f	h	a	h	l	h	l	a	f	f	f	a	h	l
Beagle	a	l	h	h	h	a	h	a	h	a	a	a	l	a	a
Black and Tan Coonhound	a	h	h	h	h	a	h	a	a	a	a	l	l	a	a
Bloodhound	a	a	h+	a	h	a	h	a	a	l	l	l	l	a	l
Borzoi	l	l	l	l	h	h	a	a	a	h	a	a	l	l	h
Dachshund	a	l	h	h	h	a	h	a	a	l	f	f	l	h	l
Foxhound, American	a	h	h	a	a	a	h	a	a	h	a	a	a	a	h
Foxhound, English	a	a	h	a	a	a	h	a	a	h	a	a	a	a	h
Greyhound	a	a	l	a	a	h	l	a	l	h	a	h	l	a	h
Harrier	a	a	h	a	a	a+	h	l	a	a	a	l	l	a	a
Irish Wolfhound	a	a	l	l	h	l	a	l	l	a+	l	l	l	h	h
Norwegian Elkhound	a	a	h	h	a	a	a	a	a	a	a	a	h	a	h
Otterhound	a	h	h	a	h	a	a	a	a	a	a	a	a	a	a
Rhodesian Ridgeback	a	a	h	a	a	l	a	a	a	a+	a	h	a	a	a
Saluki	a	a	a	a	h	h	l	h	h	l	h	a	f	a	h
Scottish Deerhound	a	a	a	l	h	a	a	a	l	a+	a	l	l	h	h
Whippet	a	a	l	a	h	h	l	h	l	h	a	h	l	a	h

The Working Breeds	Retrieving	Water retrieving	Scent discrimination	Beg	Play dead	Walk on hindq.	Sing	Push a carriage	Speaking tricks	Agility tricks	Circus tricks	Jump rope	Bark at intruders	Crawl	Jumping
Akita	l	l	l	l	h	a	a—	a	l	a	a	a	a	a	a
Alaskan Malamute	l	l	a	a	a	a	h	a	f	a	a	f	f	h	a
Bearded Collie	a+	a	h	h	h	h	a	h	h	h	a	a	a	h	h
Belgian Sheepdog	a+	a+	a+	a	a	a	a	a	a+	h	a	a	h	a	h
Belgian Tervuren	a+	a+	a+	a	a	a	a	a	a+	h	a	a	h	a	h
Belgian Malinois	a+	a+	a+	a	a	a	a	a	a+	a	a	a	h	a	a
Bernese Mountain Dog	a+	a+	h	a—	h	l	a	a	a	a	a	a	a+	a+	a
Bouvier Des Flandres	a+	a+	a+	a	a	a	a	a	a+	h	a	l	h—	h	h
Boxer	a+	a	a	a	a	a+	a	a	a+	h	a	a	a+	h	h
Briard	a+	a	a+	a	a	a	a	a	h—	h	a	a	a+	a+	h
Bull Mastiff	a	a	a	a	a	a—	a	a	a	a	a	l+	a+	a	a
Collie	a+	a+	a+	a	a	a	a	a	a+	a+	a	a	a	a	h
Corgi (Cardigan)	h—	a	a	h	a	a	a	a	a+	a	a	a	h—	a+	a—
Corgi (Pembroke)	h—	a	a	h—	a	a	a	a	a+	h	h	a	h—	a+	a—
Doberman Pinscher	a+	a+	h	a	a	a	a	a	h	h	a	a	h	h	h
German Shepherd Dog	a+	a+	h	a	a	a	a	a	h	h—	a	a	h	a	a+
Great Dane	a	a	a	a—	a	a	a	a	a	a	a	f	a	a+	a
Great Pyrenees	a	a	a	l	h	a	a	a	a	a	a	l	a+	a	a—
Komondor	a+	a+	a+	a	a	a	a	a	h	a+	a	a	h+	a	a+
Kuvasz	a+	a	a+	a	a	a	a	a	h	a+	a	a	h	a	a+
Mastiff	a	a	a—	l	a	l	a	l	a+	a	a	l	a+	a+	a
Newfoundland	a	h	a	l	a	l	a	l	a	l	l	l	a	a	a—
Puli	a+	a	a	h	a	h	a	a	h	h	h	h	a+	a+	h
Rottweiler	a+	a+	a+	a+	a	a	a+	a	h	a	a	a	h	a	a
Samoyed	a	a	a	a+	a	a	a	a	h	h	a	a	a+	a	h
Schnauzer, Giant	a+	a+	a+	a	a	a+	a	a+	h	h	a+	a	h	h	h
Schnauzer, Standard	a	a	a	a	a	a+	a	a	h	h	h	a	h	a	h
Sheepdog, Old English	a	a—	a	a	a	a	a	a	a+	a+	a	a	a	a	a+
Sheepdog, Shetland	a+	a	h	a	a	a	a	a	a+	h	a	l	a	h	h
Siberian Husky	l	l	a	a	a	a	h+	a	f	a	l	f	f	a+	a
Saint Bernard	a	a	a	l	h	l	a	a	a	a—	a—	f	a	a	a—

The Terrier Breeds	Retrieving	Water retrieving	Scent discrimination	Beg	Play dead	Walk on hindq.	Sing	Push a carriage	Speaking tricks	Agility tricks	Circus tricks	Jump rope	Bark at intruders	Crawl	Jumping
Airedale Terrier	a	a	a	a+	l	a+	a	a	h	h	h	h	a	a	h
American Staffordshire	a+	a	a	l	a	l	a	a	a	a	a	a	h	a+	a
Australian Terrier	a+	a	a+	h	a	h	a	h	h	h	a	a	a+	a	h
Bedlington Terrier	a	a	a	a	a	a	a	a	a	a	a	a	a+	a	a+
Border Terrier	h	a	h—	h	a	a	a	a	h	h	h	a	a+	h	h
Bull Terrier (White and Colored)	a+	a	a+	l	a	l	l	l	a	a—	a	h	h—	a	a—
Cairn Terrier	a	a	a+	h	a	h	a	h	h	h	h	h	h—	h	h
Dandie Dinmont	a—	a—	a	l	h	l	l	l	a	l	l	l	a—	h	l
Fox Terrier (Smooth and Wirehaired)	a	a	a	h	h—	h+	a	h	h+	h+	h+	h+	h	h	h+
Irish Terrier	a	a	a+	h	a	h	a	h	h	h	h	h	h	h	h
Kerry Blue Terrier	h	a	a	a+	a	h	a	h—	h	h	h	a	h	a	h
Lakeland Terrier	a	a	a	h	a	h	a	h	h	h	h	a	h—	a	h
Manchester Terrier	a	a	h—	a+	a	a	a	a	a+	h	h	a	a+	a	h
Norwich Terrier	a+	a	h	h	a	a	a	a	a+	a	a	a	a+	h	a
Schnauzer, Miniature	a+	a	a+	h	h	h	a	h	h	h	h	h	h—	a+	h
Scottish Terrier	a	a	a	h	a	a	a	a	h	a	a	a	h	h	a
Sealyham Terrier	a	a	h—	h	a	a	a	a	h	a	a	a	h—	h	a
Skye Terrier	a	a	a	h	h	a	a	a	h	h	a	a	a+	h—	a
Soft Coated Wheaten	a	a	h	h—	a	a	a	a	h	h	h	a	h	a	h
Staffordshire Bull	a	a	a	l	a	a	a	a	a+	a	a	a	a+	a	a
Welsh Terrier	a	a	h—	a+	a	h	a	h	h	h	h	a	h—	a	h
West Highland White	a	a	a	h	a	a	a	a	h	a	a	a	h	h	a

The Toy Breeds

	Retrieving	Water retrieving	Scent discrimination	Beg	Play dead	Walk on hindq.	Sing	Push a carriage	Speaking tricks	Agility tricks	Circus tricks	Jump rope	Bark at intruders	Crawl	Jumping
Affenpinscher	a	l	l	h	a	h	a	l	a	a	a	a	h	a	a
Chihuahua	l	l	l	l	a	l+	a	f	l	a	a	l	h+	a+	a−
Griffon, Brussels	a	a	a	h	a	a+	a	f	a	a	a	a	a+	a	a
Italian Greyhound	a	a	l	a	h	a	a	a	l	a+	a	f	f	a	h
Maltese	a	f	a	h+	h	h+	a	a	a+	a+	a	a	h	h	h
Papillon	a	a	a	a	a	a+	a	a	a	a+	a	a	a+	a	a
Pekingese	l	f	l	h	h	a+	a	a	a	l	a	l	h	a+	a−
Miniature Pinscher	a+	a	a	a	a	h	a	h−	h−	h	h	a	h	a	h
Pomeranian	a	l	a	h	h	h	h	a	a+	a+	a	a	h−	a	h
Poodle, Toy	h	h	h	h	h	h	a	h	h	h	h	a	a+	h	h
Pug	a	l	l	a	h+	a	a	a	a	a	a	f	h	a	a
Shih Tzu	a	l	l	a+	a	a	a	a	a	a−	a	l	h	h	a
Spaniel, Japanese	a	a	l	h	h	h	a	a	a	a	a	a	a+	h	a
Spaniel, English Toy	a	a	l	h	a	a	a	a	a	a	a	a	a	a	a
Terrier, Silky	a	a	h	h	a	h	a	h	h	h	a+	a	h	a	h
Terrier, Yorkshire	a	a	a	h	h	h	a	h	h−	h−	a	a	a	a	h

The Non Sporting Breeds

	Retrieving	Water retrieving	Scent discrimination	Beg	Play dead	Walk on hindq.	Sing	Push a carriage	Speaking tricks	Agility tricks	Circus tricks	Jump rope	Bark at intruders	Crawl	Jumping
Bichon Frise	a	a	a	h	a	h	a	a	a	a	a	a	a	a	a
Bulldog, English	a	l	l	f	h	l	a	f	l	f	l	f	l	a	l
Bulldog, French	a	l	l	l	h	l	a	l	a	l	l	l	a	a	l
Chow Chow	a	l	a	a	a	a	a	a	a	h	a	a	h	l	h
Dalmatian	a	a	a	h	a	h	h	h	h	h	h	h	h	a	h
Keeshond	a	a	a	h	a	h	h	h	h	h	h	h	h	h	h
Lhasa Apso	l	l	l	h	a	h	a	a	a	a	a	a	h	a	l
Poodle, Miniature	h	h	h	h	h	h	a	h	h	h	h	h	h	h	h
Poodle, Standard	h	h	h	h	h	h	a	h	h	h	h	h	h	h	h
Schipperke	a	a	a	h	a	h	a	h	h	h	a	h	h	a	a
Terrier, Boston	a	a	l	h	a	h	l	h	a	a	a	h	h	a	a
Terrier, Tibetan	a	a	a	h	a	h	a	a	h	a	a	a	h	a	a

The Last Word

As you can now see, there are some important basic differences between the obedience training you have done with your dog and the trick training you are about to begin. In obedience work, you are actually making your dog do what you ask him to do. In trick work, you usually encourage the dog to work. Most trainers will suggest that food rewards are not used in obedience work. In trick work, food rewards are encouraged—at least at the beginning. You have already established control over your dog in obedience work. Control is less important in trick work. Enthusiasm is far more important. The more wildly your dog loves to perform and the sillier he gets, the better it is for your act.

If your dog is obedience-trained and knows how to retrieve, you can pick a trick, any trick, and begin. You don't have to start with the first—start with the best—your favorite.

Whoever that whiskered, furry creature is reading over your shoulder, we wish you and him good luck and hope you both enjoy your new knowledge and newly acquired tricks and talents. Now that you've caught us in the act, we hope to catch yours one day.